The Replication of Violence

The Replication of Violence

Thoughts on International Terrorism after September 11th 2001

Suman Gupta

Pluto Press

LONDON • STERLING, VIRGINIA

First published 2002 by Pluto Press
345 Archway Road, London N6 5AA
and 22883 Quicksilver Drive,
Sterling, VA 20166–2012, USA

www.plutobooks.com

British Library Cataloguing in Publication Data
A catalogue record for this book is available from the British Library

ISBN 0 7453 1953 X hardback
ISBN 0 7453 1952 1 paperback

Library of Congress Cataloging in Publication Data
Gupta, Suman, 1966–
    The replication of violence : thoughts on international terrorism after
September 11th 2001 / Suman Gupta.
        p. cm.
Includes bibliographical references and index.
        ISBN 0–7453–1953–X (hardback) — ISBN 0–7453–1952–1 (pbk)
    1. Terrorism. 2. War on Terrorism, 2001– I. Title.
    HV6431 .G86 2002
    303.6'25—dc21
                                                        2002003705

10   9   8   7   6   5   4   3   2   1

Designed and produced for Pluto Press by
Chase Publishing Services, Fortescue, Sidmouth EX10 9QG
Typeset from disk by Stanford DTP Services, Towcester
Printed in the European Union by Antony Rowe, Chippenham, England

Contents

To all unwitting victims of political terror

Preface

I had some initial qualms about writing this book. This wasn't because I had doubts about my arguments (I know that arguments are always open to scepticism and debate). The qualms arose from the feeling that to be able to address any series of political events from a political-philosophical perspective I needed some distance from those events, some space from which to put them into relief. This seemed to be especially so for the events that I wished to address *and* in the context in which I wished to address them: those events which followed the terrorist attacks in the United States on 11 September 2001. I also wondered whether this study would get muted by other sensational and informational, reflexive and politically advocatory, books on 11 September with which readers would undoubtedly be bombarded in vast quantities.

I have persisted with this study for several reasons. One, after the terrorist attacks of 11 September I felt I was being bombarded already by the enormous quantity of images, information, opinions, political rhetoric, etc. that was conveyed to me by the mass media. Moreover, I was clearly in danger of being sucked up by the continuous discussions and debates that were humming around me – in offices, canteens, seminar rooms, streets, everywhere. Writing this was a sort of engaged withdrawal from the overwhelming intensity of the response to the attacks of 11 September and their aftermath. Two, I also felt that those images and opinions and attitudes that the mass media was bringing before me were often irresponsible and unthinking. Indeed, I felt that the very surfeit of what the mass media presented to me, and to everyone around me, was both a manifestation of this unthinkingness as well as being a manipulation of it. Undertaking this study appeared to be one way of resisting that. Three, I was curious to find out whether it is indeed possible to engage with the happening world, to address political events as they happen, from a political-philosophical perspective. I was interested in finding out why I felt it was necessary (and it is generally believed to be necessary) to be at some distance from the subject that political philosophy engages with – I have always suspected that this is a prejudice.

This study therefore has several aspects (I will leave it to the reader to decide with what success, if any, these aspects have been presented). It is a thinking record of events that took place in the period of about three months following the terrorist attacks of 11 September. It is an attempt to think through some of the concerns that surfaced in the course of that period in terms of familiar political-philosophical ideas that exist already (to do with the media, war, democracy and fanaticism, the political state, etc.). It is an attempt at demonstrating how a political-philosophical engagement with events which are yet unfolding may be undertaken. It is therefore also a reflection on the current condition and conventions of political philosophy. These, at any rate, were the ambitions. This study is naturally determined by the context in which it was written and should be read accordingly. It was done in two phases: the first five chapters were written over the month of October 2001 and finished on 1 November, and the sixth was written in the second week of December 2001 finishing on 15 December. I was in Oxford while I was working on it, with access to mass media and news resources available in Britain and other Western European countries – and the United States.

I should also clarify here that this study is not an attempt to find the causes or explanations for the terrorist attacks of 11 September. No historical material or social-cultural researches are examined for that end. I have not had access to media representations and discussions and debates that must have appeared with equal intensity in countries in the Middle East and elsewhere. I have not attempted to speculate on perspectives that might have prevailed there, or anywhere else outside the United States and Western Europe. The observations and arguments in this study are confined to and conditional on the material to which I had access.

I am grateful to my colleagues in the Literature Department of the Open University for leaving me enough time to pursue this study, and to Wolfson College Oxford for the award of a Charter Fellowship; on taking this up I was given resources and space which I have used to write this book. Thanks are also due to the centre for Research in Human Rights at the University of Surrey Roehampton for giving me access to the resources available there. I am indebted to Martin Jenkins, Joy Christian, and Xiao Cheng for making suggestions and discussing ideas which figure in it. I am grateful to Roger van Zwanenberg for supporting it and undertaking its publication, and to Anthony Winder for his painstaking editing. Any mistakes that are found in the following are my responsibility.

1 A New Kind of 'International Terrorism'

On 11 September 2001 two aeroplanes with passengers were hijacked by terrorists and crashed deliberately into the World Trade Center in New York. A similar attack was carried out on the Pentagon in Washington at roughly the same time. Between 4,000 and 6,000 people, including the terrorists, died. Amongst these were the people of some 30 nations. The news was televised around the world within a few hours of the devastation. An immense amount of space in the media has been and continues to be devoted to the most cata-strophic terrorist attack of this sort ever witnessed. Governments around the world expressed shock and regret at the tragic events, and denounced terrorism in all forms and everywhere with unpre-cedented solidarity. The United States had long harboured misgivings about the terrorist organisation, al-Quaeda, run by Osama bin Laden, who had been given refuge by the Taliban government in Afghanistan, and soon felt convinced that bin Laden was behind the terrorist attacks. The United States government, under the recently elected President George Bush and Secretary of State Colin Powell, started moves towards putting together an extraordinary coalition of governments that would aid and abet America's response to the attacks. Bush and leaders in Europe (especially Britain) were unanimous in their conviction that these terrorist attacks were a direct challenge to the 'free', democratic, 'civilised' world and 'American values'. Almost all the significant countries of the world endorsed, at least in principle, the United States's declaration of 'war against international terrorism'. Though it wasn't immediately clear what 'war against international terrorism' might entail in the long term, it was clear that in the first instance it would be an attempt to capture or kill bin Laden, get him 'dead or alive' as Bush put it. It also meant, as was made clear reasonably early, that the 'war against international terrorism' would be directed against those states that gave asylum to and sponsored terrorists, which instantly brought the Taliban-ruled Afghanistan into the firing line. Gradually it emerged that the remit of the war against terrorism could be extended to as many as 30 countries (obviously including Iraq) with alleged terrorist links, and against a wide range of organisations that could be regarded as terrorist. President Bush declared that other countries could be either 'with us or with the terrorists' in this 'first war of the twenty-first century', 'a new kind of war', a 'crusade' (all Bush's terms). On 23 September a missive allegedly from bin Laden was sent to a satellite television station in Qatar, al-Jazeereh, stating that it was the duty of everyone who professed the Islamic faith to wage a holy war against the 'American crusaders'. The consequences of these events will be all too familiar to those who read this.

This book is an attempt to come to grips with certain aspects of the phenomenon of 'international terrorism' and the connotations of a 'war against international terrorism' from a political-philosophical perspective under the shadow of these events. There has been a prodigious number of political and sociological and philosophical and international-relations-based studies of 'international terrorism' since that phrase entered the media in the late nineteen-sixties. But the events described above have brought to consciousness – have jolted – the complacency of theories that pertain to, and the existing wisdom regarding, 'international terrorism' in unexpected ways. This book is not an attempt to *explain* the momentous events of 11 September 2001 and their aftermath, but to sharpen at a broad political-philosophical level our understanding of what the connotations of 'international terrorism' and of a 'war against international terrorism' are now – or have come to be since that date. The book is the result of the jolt to theoretical complacency, to extant philosophical understanding, that the above-described events have administered – and is, therefore, necessarily under their shadow.

That however is too impressionistic a statement of the matter. A more precise approach to what this study attempts must first address the following question: what sort of jolt to philosophical understanding, to theoretical complacency, has taken place? To answer this I need to ponder the above-described events and their aftermath in more detail, and perhaps occasionally to stray into the more general concerns of political philosophy that are bound to arise in the course of such pondering. A few initial responses to that question are, it seems to me, obvious and easily summarised at the outset of this study. Before giving these however there is a matter of academic convention that needs to be briefly addressed.

It has become customary in studies of terrorism generally, and especially of the connotations of 'international terrorism' (as opposed, for instance, to 'state terrorism', 'insurgent terrorism', 'local terrorism' etc.), to acknowledge the difficulties of defining terrorism generally and particularly the attached terms. Most theoretical works that attempt to come to grips with these either take recourse to a provisional definition, or work their way through a range of inclusive definitions, after acknowledging the difficulty of finding an appropriate definition. Whatever provisional definition or range of definitions may be assumed, and there are many (often contradicting each other), there are two common denominators: that acts of terrorism involve violence against people and/or property, and that such acts are for a political purpose (where 'political' is given the broadest sense of anything impacting on a polity, and includes economic or religious or cultural motivations, agencies and outcomes). When extended to 'international terrorism' there is a third definitive denominator that comes into play: that the motives and/or agencies and/or effects of such acts cross the boundaries of nation states, and are not necessarily conducted (certainly seldom directly) at the behest of any recognised political state. It is evident however that the identification of these common denominators is not sufficient to provide sound enough grounds to be able to decide whether a particular act of political violence can be thought of as terrorist, and even if it can whether it can be clearly understood to be 'international terrorisism'. There are questions of legitimacy and perspective involved which are far more complex; there are also questions of linguistic usage and convention involved (for example, the matter of distinctions from other kinds of political violence, such as civil conflict, communal riots, war or state repression) which intervene in unexpected ways. The kinds of definition which I have alluded to are ones that seek to find an unambiguous mode of expressing *what an act of terrorism, and particularly 'international terrorism', is* – in this study, given the well-known difficulties that this approach entails, I have decided not to follow the customary path of attempting or assuming a definition or range of definitions. Instead I provisionally accept that the common denominators mentioned above give a workable, but not definitive, *sense* of the kind of act that terrorism generally, and 'international terrorism' particularly, alludes to.

More importantly, I devote much of this study to trying to understand why this difficulty of definition exists. This involves the discussion of two theses that are central to the study and that will be clarified as I progress: one, that an unambiguous understanding of *what an act of terrorism is* is hindered by the seminal consideration of *what an act of terrorism is perceived as being*, i.e. the perception of the act in this case is more illuminating than the content of that act; and two, that the idea of terrorism consequently involves a range of professed and unwitting complicities which make the issues of purpose, agency and effect unclear. The arguments that I offer in this study as a whole are constructed around and demonstrate these theses. I focus on demonstrating and giving flesh to these theses in an ongoing fashion below, rather than trying to prove them in a systematic way.

Coming back to the manner in which the events of 11 September have given a jolt to theoretical complacency, there are two obvious initial points that need to be taken into account.

One, the context of the events. If recent Western media representations of terrorism are considered (an important issue that I address in some detail very soon), it is evident that the phenomenon of terrorism has generally been presented as being primarily relevant to distant contexts which may be a matter of concern for Western countries – because of fear of contamination from outside, as affecting friendly or ideologically allied nations, or on humanitarian grounds – but seldom as being a matter for immediate anxiety. In a book aptly entitled *Civil Society and Media in Global Crises: Representing Distant Violence* (1996) (in which most of the major 'crises' of recent years are discussed, including the Gulf War and violent conflict in Kurdistan, Rwanda and Bosnia), Martin Shaw observes:

> Fundamental to establishing and maintaining distance is difference of experience. The bottom line is that wars are things that happen to non-Western people, not to us. The responses of Westerners are essentially those of the unthreatened to the plight of the threatened. This needs qualifying, however, because war – for example the bombing of civilians – is very much within the historic experience of Western societies, including personal memories of many still alive. Moreover physical threats to others in distant regions may be felt as psychological threats to Western people and undermine their sense of security. [...]
>
> Distance, psychological and even geographical, is not therefore a straightforward question. Distance is complex and relative and is constantly established, undermined and renegotiated in our

responses. Distance is active, something that we create in our response: there is *a process of distancing*. Distance is also a question, of course, of openness – in our attitudes to others' problems. We can open or close ourselves, either consciously or subconsciously, and we all move between different levels of awareness and responsiveness to a situation.[1]

Martin Shaw's sense of the complexity of distance may be justified, but the case studies he presents essentially demonstrate little more than the truth of the first two sentences. By and large distant crises are deemed such in the West because they have been represented as distant in the media (by dint of playing, in different ways, on notions of West and not-West or inside and outside, etc.), and have been accepted as distant by the usually passive media consumers (who may feel some sympathy and concern but little involvement). The sense of distance that Shaw discerns in media representations and responses to war has been on the whole true for 'international terrorism' too. Home-bred terrorism is undoubtedly a fact of life in some Western countries, but their very familiarity and locatedness keeps anxieties within limits – this is undoubtedly matter for serious concern within certain pockets, but the very fact that they are localised and oddly familiar makes them seem somehow manageable. Republican and Unionist terrorists in the United Kingdom, Basque separatists in Spain, the far-right groups that carried out the bombings in Oklahoma, the 'ethnic cleansers' of Serbia are such: they are localised within specific pockets, and worrying as they are they scare few outside those pockets and always seem to be essentially manageable in that they can be kept within bounds. The spectre of 'international terrorism', which in its very turn of phrase conjures a threat that cannot be easily managed, that seeps across boundaries and cannot be restrained and may threaten the world eventually, has been anticipated with a sort of horrified thrill by the West as a contamination that may appear (much to the glee of xenophobes and conservatives) from *outside* – from ultra-left groups, from Islamic fundamentalist groups – but still reassuringly *outside*. This has been underlined by a sense of complacency about the numerical difference in incidences of terrorism generally within the West and outside. The number of civil conflicts and correlated incidences of terrorism in Africa, Asia, and South America seemed to far outweigh the number of such conflicts and consequent terrorism within North America and Europe. 'International terrorism' may have been mooted as the post-Cold-War world threat for at least two decades and may have been a matter for political debate and legislation along conservative lines, but it has been perceived as being psychologically and even geographically distant – something *outside* – on the verge of being a B-movie fantasy or as remote a possibility as an alien invasion or an asteroid crashing into Earth. The very exaggerated imagining and visualisation of successful and near-catastrophic 'international terrorist' activity within the West (the province of numberless indifferent Hollywood films) had concretised that sense of distance. That 'international terrorist' acts have now *actually materialised with such all-too-tangible effect within the Western context* is a substantial shock: 'international terrorism' appears to have suddenly become more than a xenophobe's or conservative's nightmare or a media fad or a Hollywood fantasy, it appears to have become a serious and urgent and in some sense *within-our-zone* affair crying out for renewed academic assessment and a concerted political effort. And yet this sudden flipping of perspective that acts of 'international terrorism' *within the Western context* has brought about is not simply a reversal: it is not simply the case that that which seemed somewhat far-fetched and fantastical before has proved to be quite real and tangible; instead the realm of the real and tangible has itself become indistinguishable from the fantastical and far-fetched. Too many scare-mongering theories and Hollywood fantasies that were reassuringly distant have simply moved in close, become real, without wholly losing the almost-virtual veneer. This complex blurring of distinctions between what was perceived as plausible and implausible, as the exaggerated and the down-to-earth, initiated quite simply by the *context* of the 11 September events, is itself reason enough to revisit the theoretical ground on which 'international terrorism' has been largely discussed.

Two, the scale of the casualties. One of the familiar arguments of political theorists on the left has been that the perceived threat of modern 'international terrorism' in the West, which was initially, and rather mendaciously, touted as something that emanates primarily from the East with the support of Communist governments, has since the end of the Cold War been systematically heightened and played up and given as the prerogative primarily of Islamic fundamentalists, and sometimes of ultranationalist movements in the Third World and 'rogue states', to keep a crisis mentality alive. This has allowed Western governments to maintain controlling interests outside their dominions, and to keep afloat an

economy which is heavily geared towards defence budgeting –
ultimately with a view to maximising capitalist interests by securing
markets and favourable trade agreements. The alleged rise of 'international terrorism', so the argument went, is actually chimerical.
That this threat from terrorism is being exaggerated is amply evident
in the fact that the actual scale of casualties and damage arising from
'international terrorist' acts does not merit the kind of attention it
has received from politicians and the media. In an essay entitled *The
Future of Terrorism* (1997), for example, Conor Gearty took this line:

> Without any great war or massive insurgency to distract us, we
> have been able to indulge our anxieties about the terrorists'
> sporadic violence. Concern about 'terrorism' in the West is
> therefore paradoxically reassuring, since contriving the level of
> passion could only be possible in a time of relative peace. The
> point can be reinforced by considering exactly how much of this
> political violence there has been during this 'age of terrorism'. The
> evidence is complicated by difficulties of definition, but whatever
> yardstick is chosen the numbers of casualties remain historically
> extremely low. If we restrict ourselves to political violence which
> crosses boundaries or is otherwise international in character, the
> figure for the number of fatalities since the 1960s is on any
> statistical basis in the low thousands. Certainly there has been no
> year in which any agency, think-tank or research group, no matter
> how enthusiastically or expansively it has defined the subject, has
> ever managed to find more than a thousand fatalities a year from
> 'international terrorism'.[2]

A wealth of statistics and figures, including FBI estimates, supported
Conor Gearty's observations about the historically comparatively
low quantity of 'international terrorism' casualties of recent years.
Even the most intrepid statisticians with an inclination to justify the
fear of 'international terrorism' had to resort to speculative figures to
make their point. Such are the efforts of Todd Sandler and Walter
Enders in 'Is Transnational Terrorism Becoming More Threatening?'
(2000); they go through a complicated statistical exercise to come
up with the following counterintuitive conclusion:

> Despite a decline in transnational terrorism of nearly 50 incidents
> per quarter during some of the post-cold war era, terrorism still
> presents a formidable threat to targets. This conclusion follows

because each incident is almost 17 percentage points more likely to result in death or injury compared with the previous decades.[3]

The argument that Gearty presented in this quantitative fashion however goes further. In books written in and since the nineteen-eighties (starting with Noam Chomsky and Edward S. Herman)[4] it was convincingly demonstrated that the Western media, consciously or otherwise, downplay or reinterpret in positive ways acts which could be thought of as terroristic which happen to be perpetrated by the United States or by her allies and with her support, and play up acts which are against the interests of the United States or her allies, seeing them as terroristic even when they could have been understood as undertaken for emancipatory purposes. The irony is, as these studies show, that acts which have led to widespread terror, but have not been brought under the banner of 'international terrorism' in the Western media, are usually at the instance of the United States and her allies – and are quantitatively far larger than those that were presented as being terrorist. A systematic examination of the way United States foreign policy developed during the Cold War and has been conducted since the end thereof leads Chomsky to conclude (a matter I come back to in Chapter 5) that '[I]n plain English, U.S. violence, terror, robbery, and exploitation will be able to proceed without the annoying impediments portrayed as the Kremlin's 'global designs' in the official culture.'[5] In this context the significance of the scale of casualties in the 11 September terrorist attacks can hardly be overlooked. Both the linked arguments outlined briefly above – the chimerical character of what officially passes for 'international terrorism' in the West and behind that the shrouded character of the United States's and her allies' 'state terrorism' – can be countered by the emotional impact of the scale of casualties. The scale of casualties is a matter not just of the number of those killed, but also of the number of those who are bereaved. The scale of casualties incorporates within itself the impact of being comparable to other conflicts that figure prominently in the history of the United States: media reports included plenty of comparisons with Pearl Harbor bombings and the Civil War. The scale of casualties also incorporates within itself the association of those killed with the locations in which they died: the potent symbolism of the World Trade Center (international capitalism) and the Pentagon (United States military might) rubs off on all those who constitute that scale of casualties. By association the contemplation of the scale of casualties acquires a certain symbolic potency: it becomes an enormous attack against the United States itself, against 'American values'. By similar kinds of symbolic association the contemplation of the scale of casualties has been perceived as not just an attack on the United States and 'American values' in abstract, but on the West at large and 'Western values' in abstract. The scale of casualties is materially such that it involves people not just of United States nationality, but of a large number of other Western and non-Western nationalities too. In the emotional impact of the contemplation of the scale of casualties, with the perception of this being an attack on the United States and the West and their values, the sense of sharing bereavement can be drawn on in interestingly derivative ways. Most major European countries could claim a significant number of casualties (in the British media, for instance, the 200 suspected British casualties had initially figured significantly, though later that fell to around 50). At the same time the significant numbers of South American and Chinese and Indian and, for that matter, Middle Eastern people (with the British and United States media as my main channels of information, I have found it difficult to gauge precise figures in this regard) who probably figure within that scale of casualties could be conveniently overlooked. By derivation, in other words, the scale of casualties has become attached primarily to Northern American and wholly Western civilians; the scale of casualties indicates an enormous act of aggression of which the United States and the West are the *victims*. The perception of being victims makes the perception of being perpetrators, as Chomsky has often argued (obviously never a comfortable perception within the West), seem like an outrage in itself.

Both the distinguishing features of the events of 11 September 2001 – the context in which it occurred and the scale of casualties – have clearly given a substantial jolt to theoretical perspectives of 'international terrorism'. The sense of distance with which such theorisation has been conducted in recent years, especially within a dominant Western academy, is suddenly eroded. The mediating channels of the media and popular modes of entertainment – that had, often while apparently raising consciousness of the threat of 'international terrorism' towards the West, actually underlined its distance by drawing the imagining of 'international terrorist' acts within the sphere of ill-supported conspiracy theories and superlative rhetoric and the fantastic – have suddenly redefined their mediatory roles. The sense that the real and the fantastic, the superlative and the immediately actual, have somehow merged with each other and grown indistinguishable is itself a matter with which political and cultural theory needs to come to grips. Crucially, the effects of the context, combined with the psychological effect of the scale of casualties and the symbolism that has accrued around this, has apparently undermined some carefully researched and validated theoretical positions that the left (in an uncompromising fashion) and certain liberals (in a conciliatory fashion) had taken seriously. In one fell swoop on 11 September those who could be perceived as perpetrators (the West) and their allies had turned into victims, and those who could be conceived of as victims (the objects of Western power politics and self-interest) had turned into perpetrators. The chimera of world fanaticism and 'international terrorism' promoted by the dominant Western powers has apparently proved to be not so chimerical after all. The exaggerated rhetoric and self-righteousness (which any systematic examination of history and contemporary politics could throw into doubt) of conservatives and right-oriented factions within the West, to whose propagandist efforts the Western electorate has over the years often proved to be sympathetic, have suddenly acquired a certain concrete validity. Liberals within the West, whose politics (which has been gaining ground among Western electorates) sought to find a mediating position, a Third Way, between left and right, while maintaining some open-mindedness regarding what the role of the West has been in the past and how it should proceed hereafter, find that accepting the conservative position (always with a humanitarian liberal gesture or two) is easier since 11 September. Politically the left had been left out in the cold by the Western electorate since the end of the Cold War, but at least increasingly popular liberal sympathies had continued to take leftist perspectives seriously. After 11 September the left has moved from out into the cold to way into deep freeze. A few muted pacifist voices – some student marches (no one has taken students and universities seriously in the West since the sixties) and some unnoticed peace demonstrations – were almost all that remained. The leftists continued to make their points: that American foreign policy and European collaboration has to some extent *produced* this terrorist act, that in the process of feeling victimised and outraged an endemic xenophobia in the West is becoming officially ensconced, that if anything could make the situation worse for all and more favourable for those who thrive on violence it would be an excessive

United-States-led reprisal, etc. Liberals continued to respond to the flavour of truth in these observations with sympathetic gestures and qualified approval, and it is clear that such gestures will carry on being made, but the whole left-perspective business is now understood to be ineffective and therefore irrelevant. Let the gestures be made (it redounds to the West's virtue that they should be allowed, it is felt) – but it is clear to all that suddenly all those weak and war-ridden and ravaged theocracies and tyrannies that the West loved to hate, and pointed to partly in a kind of indifferent pity and partly with a sense of self-congratulatory satisfaction, and mostly to determine whether they can be exploited in any way, had grown into an indistinct and yet paradoxically coherent and enormous monster with a shadow that loomed over a now embattled and careworn West. The West had its own victims and body bags.

Following the events of 11 September in New York and Washington, attitudes to and perspectives regarding 'international terrorism' have undoubtedly changed. For those with an interest in coming to grips with these changes and the connotations of 'international terrorism' and of a 'war against international terrorism' now it is necessary to start with some theoretical basics (despite the Thatcherite inflection of that, I do not intend to presume a left or right or centre position). This book is devoted to some of these theoretical basics pertinent to 'international terrorism' and a 'war against international terrorism' after 11 September.

2 'International Terrorism' as a Media Event

In an interview shortly after 11 September (the remarks were reported on the 19th) the highly regarded German composer Karlheinz Stockhausen made the following comment on the terrorist attacks:

> What happened there is – they all have to rearrange their brains now – is the greatest work of art ever.
>
> That characters can bring about in one act what we in music cannot dream of, that people practise madly for ten years, completely fanatically, for a concert and then die. That is the greatest work of art for the whole cosmos. Against that, we, composers, are nothing.[1]

The remarks received a fair amount of attention in the European media. People in Germany and elsewhere were outraged at what was perceived as Stockhausen's lack of sensitivity and indifference to human life. A couple of his concerts were cancelled, organisers of the Hamburg Festival withdrew their invitation to the distinguished composer, the Barbican management had to publicly defend its decision to retain Stockhausen recitals in its calendar. Stockhausen apologised for the remarks, said that he had not meant to offend anyone and that his words had been taken out of context and misunderstood, and explained that he had meant to compare the attacks to 'a production of the devil, Lucifer's work of art'.

In common-sense terms the statement quoted above does sound like profound and callous nonsense – however there are some ways in which, taken out of context as it is, it may make some sense. It could, for instance, be taken as an assertion of the amorality and discreteness of art (roughly along Oscar Wildean lines). The idea could be that *if that terrorist act is perceived as a work of art*, then, irrespective of the moral outrage that it might arouse, we would have to acknowledge that it is a great work of art given the enormity of it. Or, alternatively, it could merely be a speculation from an artistic point of view: for an artist any act, however unpalatable, can be seen as the subject of inspiration (even the Holocaust can lead to creativity). Or, perhaps, this suggests that any act that changes perceptions of normality and ordinary life has something akin to the effect of a work of art in it. However that statement may be understood though, there is the unavoidable premise: that, at some level, the terrorist attack had been dissociated from its causes and consequences and become, for Stockhausen, a discrete act-in-itself, something like an unfamiliar image or a first performance never seen before. There is the audience ('they all' who have to reorient themselves), the 'one act' that is the culmination, the self-annihilating artists (presumably the terrorists and their unfortunate victims). This itself is extraordinary. If considered cold-bloodedly, it must be admitted that Stockhausen's impression of something uncontextualised and finished and somehow distant – like an unfamiliar photograph or a first performance – is something that most of us do share at some level. The manner in which the terrorist acts of 11 September were encountered by the larger part of the world (those who weren't perpetrators or victims, or their relatives and friends and acquaintances, or simply bystanders in New York and Washington) did resonate with something of Stockhausen's sense of dissociation. For most of the people of the world who paid attention (I think that in different ways most did) the events of 11 September were mediated by the mass media: were constructed and reconstructed and re-reconstructed out of the inflections of tone and delivery of newsreaders on the radio, by the stylistically nuanced texts of newspapers, by the reported voices of those involved in different ways in the disaster, and most potently by the still and moving photographs of two aeroplanes crashing, in a sort of fatalistic silence, into the two towers of the World Trade Center (replicated endlessly, from different directions, in slow and fast motion, from close up and from a distance, juxtaposed in various ways with other pictures from before and after, contextualised each time by different commentaries and reactions).

Much as we – anyone who reads this – might hate to admit it, the mediation of the mass media and the distancing effect it has on our view of the world is an unavoidable condition; an unavoidable condition which clashes ironically with the most obvious aspect of the very symbolism of the terrorist attacks of 11 September. Most obviously, the attacks did violence to the most potent symbols of a consumer society, striking at the very heart of the institutions that valorise and protect consumerism. The fact is that that violence itself got converted at the selfsame moment, despite our resistance and horror, into consumable images following the irresistible logic of mass-media representation; the violence crudely aimed at the consumer society became food to that consumer society. In some essential way our response to an image of such immense violence mediated by the mass media is tendentiously what Baudrillard would call a 'misrecognition', which gets perpetuated if we admit it (perhaps unwittingly Stockhausen has simply admitted it) and which gets perpetuated if we refuse to admit it (marked by the sense of triviality and theatricality in those who objected so vociferously and self-righteously to Stockhausen's unhappy remarks):

> So we live, sheltered by signs, in the denial of the real. A miraculous security: when we look at the images of the world, who can distinguish this brief irruption of reality from the profound pleasure of not being there? The image, the sign, the message – all these things we 'consume' – represent our tranquillity consecrated by distance from the world, a distance more comforted by the allusion to the real (even when the allusion is violent) than compromised by it.
>
> The content of the messages, the signifieds of the sign, are largely immaterial. We are not engaged in them, and the media do not involve us in the world, but offer for our consumption signs as signs, albeit signs accredited with the guarantee of the real. It is here that we can define *the praxis of consumption*. The consumer's relation to the real world, to politics, to history, to culture is not a relation of interest, investment or committed responsibility – nor is it one of total indifference: it is a relation of **curiosity**. On the same pattern, we can say that the dimension of consumption as we have defined it here is not one of knowledge of the now, nor one of total ignorance: it is the dimension of **misrecognition**.[2]

In the wake of the 11 September terrorist attacks I think it was immediately evident that these were first and foremost a media event, unavoidably distant to the larger part of the world in being expeditiously and repetitively conveyed to it in the mass media, prone to an inevitable Baudrillardian 'misrecognition'. Equally the degree of the violence, the dim recognition of the brutal reality distanced by this 'misrecognition', forced many consumers to rebel against the 'misrecognition' – to acknowledge the brutal reality all the more passionately or humanely or thoughtfully. But that very acknowledgement itself got caught in the mass-media machine, as an act of good faith to what was happening but more necessarily to cater to ever more consumption. The terrorist attacks, it was reported, had brought even the most obdurately provincial to television screens: those who usually follow the news on television and newspapers began to follow it even more closely, those who seldom did more than catch the news on television began to buy newspapers, those who were largely indifferent to the news began to turn at least to the television broadcasts. The acknowledgement of the brutal reality which was supposed to defeat the inevitable 'misrecognition' was itself a 'misrecognition', a consuming curiosity, exacerbated by the theatre and theatricality of the political manoeuvres that followed – on the mass media.

But this terrorist attack had opened up a fissure of some sort that only succeeded in closing in upon itself. This terrorist attack, by its enormity and by the context within which it occurred, had managed to turn the attention of the media and its relation to extreme violence (an unavoidable reality) upon itself. Media consumers had now, I think inevitably, an inkling of their complicity in the *production* of media violence, had faced their discomfort with this complicity, and had ultimately surrendered to the complicity.

Two tasks arise out of these observations. One, it is necessary to reassess the relationship between the media and 'international terrorism'; two, it is necessary to peel away the layers of media representation that cover 'international terrorism' and get to the core of the matter (that question: what is 'international terrorism' apart from being a media event?).

Serious discussions of the relationship that an increasingly extensive and better-coordinated international mass media has to the threat of 'international terrorism' seems to have been initiated in the nineteen-seventies. Several influential works on terrorism at the time emphatically asserted that the international mass media had become an instrument that could be appropriated by terrorists to extend the impact of terrorism and to promote the purposes underlying such activity.[3] The various uses to which the media could be put by terrorists was summarised admirably by Amy Sands Redlick in an essay on 'The Transnational Flow of Information as a Cause of Terrorism' (1979):

Informational flows [...] seem to benefit militants or discontented individuals or groups in today's international system in four main ways. First, mass media coverage of an event will lead to greater attention, even if momentary, being given to individuals or groups involved and their reasons for causing such a controversy. In this sense, it is a propaganda tool. Second, the flow of information may expose societies to information that will inspire and justify an individual's or group's use of violence. Third, by providing information concerning specific terrorist tactics and strategies, the international communications system has often supplied discontented groups sufficient technological knowledge and ideological justification to support their use of terrorism. Fourth, the flow of information resulting from a successful terrorist attack may provide the utilitarian inspiration needed to cause a contagion of similar events elsewhere in the world.[4]

A more sophisticated version of this approach to the mass media as a kind of organ for terrorist propaganda and an instrument of terrorist activity was developed in Alex P. Schmid and Janny de Graaf's *Violence as Communication* (1982), though they confined themselves ostensibly to what they called 'insurgent terrorism' ('social-revolutionary, separatist and single issue terrorism aiming at the top of society').[5] This limitation in Schmid and de Graaf's study seems to leave out the less predictable and indistinctly located field of 'international terrorism', but is in fact relevant to this too in offering a particularly interesting definition of terrorism which I address soon. The view that the mass media is in some sense a useful instrument for terrorists is one that has been repeated ad nauseam since the nineteen-seventies, seems to be a matter of common sense, and continues to enjoy some academic currency.[6] If this view is accepted the mass media itself becomes the focus of counter-terrorist restrictions. This is problematic, as most of those who subscribe to the terrorist's-instrument understanding of the mass media acknowledge: the importance of disseminating information on terrorist acts (to enable people to assess the situation for themselves, and to justify such measures as a government may be obliged to take as a result of such acts) cannot be gainsaid, and the principle of freedom of information is generally understood to be consistent with civil liberty and democratic choice. Nevertheless, from this perspective it does become necessary to consider what sort of controlling measures may be adopted with regard to the mass media as an indirect way of controlling the effectiveness of terrorist acts. This has ranged from straightforward censorship of certain sorts, to hoping that the press would regulate itself in a responsible and aware fashion, to recommending that independent bodies be set up that would ensure a balance between responsible reporting and the freedom of the press.[7] This leads however to the flip side of the above approach: that the mass media could be and has been used as the instrument of the state to mendaciously manipulate consumers towards certain ideological positions from which it becomes possible to justify the most unpalatable of state activities (acts of 'state terrorism' on a national and international scale) and to present oppositional or alternative ideological positions as unacceptable or wrong. This could be effected by direct state control of media resources, but also in circumstances where the media enjoy apparent freedom by the fact that political states are necessarily the pre-eminent information and analysis providers, control other ideological sensitive areas which impinge on media representation (education, the economy, etc.), and have extensive legislative powers which can affect the media directly or indirectly. The view of the mass media as the instrument of the state was most powerfully argued by Edward S. Herman in *The Real Terror Network* (1982) in the first instance and has been discussed by others since.[8] Some of the associated arguments that arise from this approach have been outlined already in the introduction.

Empirically based research which tries to validate these positions and expectations by taking sample responses to particular media representations from cross-sections of consumers (a self-evidently limited methodology) has led to inconclusive observations. A study along these lines of responses to television representations of terrorist activity in Britain by Schlesinger, Murdock and Elliott, *Televising Terrorism* (1983), for instance, found that media representations of terrorism and responses to them are more diverse than either of the above-mentioned approaches suggests.[9] Similar conclusions have since been reached by a range of empirically based studies pertinent to a range of different contexts. However, such empirical studies are limited by their means. A systematic examination of a range of specific media representations and representative responses (which can then be grouped into categories in terms of class, education, ethnicity, gender, etc.) can arguably indicate to what degree psychological and informational effects can be demonstrated to have taken place. But empirical studies are unlikely to be material to the notion that the media are controlled by the state in complex ways, in that the simple examination of particular representations and responses (which would not, in any case, necessarily be aware of the manner in which ideological state apparatuses and ideological manipulation may be at work) is unlikely to throw much light upon a tendency toward broad ideological conformity and manipulation, despite a range of individual and categorical differences. To validate or invalidate the latter approach by empirical means necessitates a broader view of sociological and historical processes than empirical studies are likely to be able to accommodate, and a more extensive empirical basis than is normally feasible. Careful empirical studies can also occasionally fail to determine, even within the constraints of their material, significant relationships between media representation and responses to particular terrorist acts, and have then to extend to more speculative reasoning to understand their results. An instructive instance of this is found in Carol W. Lewis's examination of public responses to the Oklahoma bombings in 1996 ('The Terror that Failed: Public Opinion in the Aftermath of the Bombing in Oklahoma City' (2000)), which finds that despite substantial media coverage and discussion the bombings had in fact not particularly affected the public.[10] This can however be promptly responded to by other equally empirically-based studies, such as Michelle Slone's 'Responses to Media Coverage of Terrorism' (2000), in which it is found that the mass media representation of terrorism and political violence definitely 'has an impact on the psychological well-being' of consumers, though the nature of the reactions varies according to religiousness, tendency to be dogmatic, and gender.[11]

Finally, a perspective regarding the role of the media in situations of international crisis (though excluding terrorism), which has been gaining currency through the nineteen-nineties, should also be mentioned, since this may be thought of as providing an alternative to the instrumentalist perspective of the mass media that all the above-mentioned arguments assume. According to this perspective, the mass media could under certain circumstances play a determinative, rather than instrumental, role in the foreign policy of different governments and in international politics. This, it is argued, is especially evidenced in crisis conditions when governments have been forced to offer humanitarian aid to crisis-struck countries and to negotiate international policy in benign directions because of media exposure of the public to conditions on the ground. Such a line of argument had been presented with some success by N. Gowing in 'Real-Time Television Coverage of Armed Conflicts and Diplomatic Crises' (1994).[12] The understanding of the media as an independent and determinative political agent has since been emphasised and elaborated elsewhere.[13] Pertinent as this may seem to the above discussion, I feel that it doesn't actually have a bearing on the special case of the international mass media's relationship to 'international terrorism': the mass media have in almost all instances involving political violence which could, by some definition, be thought of as 'international terrorism' been unambiguously (though variably) aligned with an extrinsic political position (usually a state-determined one, rarely an oppositional one).[14] In the context of representing 'international terrorism' the mass media seem to play an essentially instrumentalist role.

What this background of thinking in recent years demonstrates about the relationship of the international mass media to terrorism is the degree to which the media are unequal to coping with events such as those of 11 September. How the events of 11 September have affected views from the left (the media as a tool of the state), such as Herman's and Chomsky's, I have already discussed briefly in Chaper 1. More importantly, these terrorist attacks have also revealed the inadequacies of more conservative academic approaches to the issue. If we go back momentarily to those four ways in which, according to Redlick (quoted above), international information flows may assist terrorism, it is evident that the first two and the fourth are not valid in this instance. It seems to me self-evident that these particular terrorist attacks were not intended for propaganda for the political views of a particular group, or to inspire others to use such tactics in support of their views. There is one crucial factor here: no one (or no one who could be seriously believed) actually *claimed* responsibility for the acts after the event. It is received wisdom from those who have considered this matter that where propaganda and inspiration are the objects, claiming responsibility is a matter of prime importance.[15] In this case responsibility had been *attributed* rather than *claimed*. It is also received wisdom that for propaganda and inspiration in Redlick's sense, the thrust of the terrorist attack (as Laqueur among others has observed)[16] is on the character and appropriateness of the target, rather than the scale of casualties. In these attacks the scale of casualties is certainly the first thing that leaps to mind – much more so than the crude symbolism of the buildings targeted. The targets and the timing of these attacks were chosen to cause the maximum and most indiscriminate loss of human life. The tragic and pathetic celebrations at these events in Palestine that were seen on television were exceptional: everywhere, including the Middle East, it was immediately apparent that these were terrible events that would have terrible repercussions which could not possibly be welcomed by ordinary people anywhere. Even Redlick's third mode of terrorist use of the media doesn't apply here: I don't think these terrorist attacks could be considered as showing a new method of death dealing. It was reported shortly after the attacks that the reputed international terrorist who goes popularly under the name of Carlos the Jackal (Ilich Ramirez Sanchez) and resides in a French prison has stated that the technique – using aeroplanes as bombs to target buildings – had in fact been discussed in terrorist circles in 1991. The simplicity of the technique, a combination of hijacking and suicide bombing, is such that it would be very strange indeed if those who make political violence their business had not thought of it before. If such techniques have not been used before it seems to me that this is for one reason: it needs a kind of absolute brutality, a kind of single-minded and calculated will to mass killing, which is extremely rare outside a declared war situation and would in most conceivable circumstances be considered politically counterproductive.

The events of 11 September defeat familiar modes of understanding the media's relationship to terrorism.

What the international mass media were faced with in the first instance, and continued to grapple with for some time, was the task of representing a media event of gigantic proportions without any apparent frame, without any clear comprehension of perpetrator, purpose or effect – an event that had enormous political and human significance but with few indications about how to frame that significance and put it into perspective. It was a media event that appeared with phenomenological starkness. That undoubtedly is why media representations of the events of 11 September and their aftermath threatened to reveal the nature of mass media itself, bringing to the surface the danger and anxiety of 'misrecognition' in a Baudrillardian sense instead of falling in with a comfortable and unavoidable habit of 'misrecognition'. That is why Stockhausen's remarks both struck a chord and provoked outrage.

The mass media have naturally responded to this unusual task by focusing on retrospective reconstruction in certain directions that do not in fact yet frame the terrorist attacks convincingly. Instead the mass media have more or less *created* a fragile frame by a method of constant fittings and refittings, by repetition and adjustment, by blurring distinctions and then drawing out particularities from the blur, by a process of throwing up a surfeit of connected but incoherent information and then adding to these and gradually letting a few ideas take dominance, and most importantly by constantly trying to gauge and accommodate to the pulse of political opinion and consumer demand within the West (where the heart of the international mass media lies). To understand this I go back to a mode of trying to grasp the relationship of the mass media to terrorism that, despite its limitations, seem to me to be pertinent to the situation that concerns us now. To be precise, I go back to Schmid and de Graaf's unusual definition of terrorism in *Violence as Communication*, which is ostensibly limited to 'insurgent terrorism' and which is known to have substantial conceptual problems[17] – nevertheless, that definition in itself is worth reconsidering:

> We [...] define terrorism as *the deliberate and systematic use or threat of violence against instrumental (human) targets (C) in a conflict between two (A, B) or more parties, whereby the immediate victims C – who might not even be part of the conflicting parties – cannot, through a change of attitude or behaviour, dissociate themselves from the conflict.* Since the aim of terrorism is behaviour modification of the enemy and/or public and not of the immediate victims, a certain arbitrariness in the selection of the instrumental targets is characteristic of the terrorist form of violence.[18]

This provides a useful terminology for understanding the reaction of the mass media to the terrorist attacks of 11 September. The problem here is that the parties of the conflict were hazy. It was difficult to say *who, why and what* was A – the terrorists who had, so to say, communicated through this act. This was not just a matter of apportioning blame to the unambiguously identified source of the attacks, though that in itself was a significant consideration. Apportioning blame had to be done retrospectively here and inevitably had a hint, however slight, of uncertainty. There seemed to be little doubt that some extremist Islamic group was responsible, that this group was somehow connected (probably directly) to bin Laden and his organisation. And yet there was uneasiness about this certainty, uneasiness about the glibness with which this certainty seemed to be reached: there had been so much unmerited discussion and propaganda about the threat of Islamic extremist terrorism that one wondered whether this apportioning of blame under such circumstances wasn't too prepared; there was at the time so little hard evidence to consider and so much to be taken on trust from United States intelligence sources, who had failed anyway, that one couldn't help but worry a little; there was so much doubt about what can unanimously be considered to be conclusive evidence anyway that it seemed difficult to take a principled stand on this; there was the nagging thought that such apportioning of blame had happened after the Oklahoma bombings but was proved wrong, and that no one in this instance had once thought of far right groups within the United States (they would have been wrong, of course) who are just as anti-democracy and anti-freedom and anti-capitalism as any extremist ... But the haziness of A was not just a matter of identification, it was also a matter of motive (Why do this? To what end? With what calculation?) and a matter of extent (In what way are they distinct from other extreme religious and political groups? What may A do next?). The haziness of A was echoed in the haziness of B – the protective state which had, so to speak, received the act of communication that had taken place in this act. Here the identity seemed clear: the United States and what she 'believes in' and 'stands for'. But again the uncertainties began to creep in, a blurred aura appeared around that clear identification: what is it that the United States 'believes in' and 'stands for'? Is it what she claims to believe in and stand for through her statesmen (freedom, democracy, etc.)? But so many different political states claim exactly those beliefs, and if this attack was on those beliefs then surely it was not confined to the United States? And everyone with a slight interest in world politics since the Second World War was aware that the virtues that the United States so proprietorially claims have not in fact always been adhered to by her – more often than not if one gets down to details. It was clear that, even while decisively accepting the role of B, the United States was floundering in the face of the haziness of A, was turning rather hazy herself. The United States had increasingly in this context become an abstraction – an abstraction of goodness and virtue to herself and her staunchest allies, an abstraction of duplicity and double standards to sceptics – but nothing more concrete than an abstraction. And to the United States as B, A, the perpetrator, was also (despite the certainty of this being the handiwork of extremist Islamic groups under the demagogic influence of bin Laden and like-minded monsters) no more concrete than an abstraction, a wraith, nothing less than *terrorism itself*. The clash of A and B that was announced through this terrible terrorist act was no more than a clash of indistinct, hazy, decontextualised –

and let's face it, deeply worrying – abstractions: 'good against evil' (Bush said that); freedom and democracy itself against fanaticism and terrorism itself (Bush, Blair and many others); and (with a pinch of mindless xenophobia thrown in) the Western world, with its Christian roots, against the uncivilised Islamic world, a 'clash of civilisations' no less (Italian Premier Berlusconi *said* that amidst moderate shock and disbelief, but Bush had already implied it with his 'crusade'). The only certainty in this act of terrorist communication was its 'instrumental target', that which Schmid and de Graaf label C – the 4,000 to 6,000 people who had died and those who mourned them.

Seen in this fashion one can understand why the mass media faced difficulty in framing these events. The clash of abstractions could be thought of as 'the change of attitude and behaviour', 'the behaviour modification of the enemy and/or the public' that Schmid and de Graaf mention in their definition. What the international mass media were obliged to do under these peculiar circumstances, under the (no doubt transitory) pressure of the anxiety of knowing their own habit of 'misrecognition' amongst consumers, faced with the phenomenological starkness of the images of mass destruction on 11 September 2001 in New York and Washington, was carefully and searchingly to transmit the behavioural modifications, the gradual process of abstractions taking flesh and becoming something meaningful and coalescing into some sort of fragile frame. The posturings of political leaders who felt something needed to be done, the sad flounderings of those who were caught in the zone of reprisals (especially Pakistan), the fearful and scary rhetoric of an Islamic clerisy which found the faith itself threatened, the optimism of other leaders who had been suffering from their own terrorist problems and hoped their terrorists could be lumped into this clash of abstractions (Israel, India), the emotive outpourings of academics and writers of every description in the West, photographs of the expressionless faces of the immediate perpetrators – looking quite ordinary – shrouded forever in mystery, images of hapless relatives of the victims looking for them, snippets of gossip about who is saying what, breathless jots of information about the behaviour of markets ... all these flowed across television and computer screens and newspaper pages, getting juxtaposed, getting sorted, getting memorised and forgotten, in a massive dynamic of charting changes in behaviour and attitudes after 11 September. Out of this dynamic gradually emerged the unstable clash of abstractions.

That is what the international mass media had made of the events of 11 September which are now understood to be the quintessential manifestation of 'international terrorism'. To get behind that we need to go behind the mere surface of the mass media event itself, to go into those very abstractions themselves. That, of course, is what I hope to do in the rest of this study.

On 28 September it was reported that the well-known director Woody Allen 'described the terror attacks on New York as "fair game" for any artist with an insight to offer into the tragedy'.[19]

3 Terrorism as War and War Against Terrorism

After the terrorist attacks of 11 September the United States declared 'war against international terrorism'. This, it was declared, would be a long and costly war involving a large number of different countries (both as targets and within an alliance, though details remained vague) and conducted on a range of different fronts (intelligence, direct military action, diplomatic procedures, etc.). Most immediately it seemed, however, that it would be a fairly straightforward attack on the Taliban government in Afghanistan, which was charged with giving refuge to bin Laden and his al-Quaeda network. This probably wasn't considered an especially controversial first step; after all, the ultrapuritanical Islamic state that the Taliban were trying to institute involved appalling violations of human rights and civil rights, and the Taliban had few allies. Moreover Afghanistan had already been ravaged by prolonged war and instability during and since the Soviet occupation. NATO members as such, and countries in the West independently, had offered their unconditional support in the 'war against international terrorism', and efforts were initiated to recruit an international coalition for that purpose. As the process drew out and it increasingly seemed as if 'war against international terrorism' might not consist of much more than an attack on Taliban-controlled Afghanistan and the 'taking out' of bin Laden, it became clear that support wouldn't be as unqualified as it had initially seemed even from those at the heart of Western Europe (not to speak of the Arab world). It was reported that the French Prime Minister Lionel Jospin was uncomfortable about the 'war against international terrorism' being understood as a 'war against Islam'. German Chancellor Gerhard Schroeder expressed a certain reluctance to support military actions which were not measured and well considered, and expressed a distaste for 'American adventures'. British Prime Minister Tony Blair continued, as expected, to pledge staunch support for all kinds of American retaliatory actions, while simultaneously trying to placate an anxious Muslim community in Britain and offering humanitarian aid to Afghan refugees. On the whole the Western coalition in the 'war against international terrorism' held, but the search for coalition partners within Asia proved more complicated. All political states expressed sympathy with the United States and her victims, but direct military assistance was another matter. The United States could generally depend on Israel but there was still the sticky problem of Israel–Palestine hostilities, which had been escalating steadily before 11 September. A fragile Israel–Palestine ceasefire was organised, but suspicions and doubts marred this respite on both sides and soon it collapsed altogether. China and Russia (with the satellite central Asian republics) expressed willingness to support military action but were reluctant to offer air bases for the purpose or other material assistance. Iran expressed sympathy with the victims of the terrorist attacks and later warned the United States that any infringement of air space in the course of retaliatory action against Afghanistan would bring about retaliatory action in turn. Saudi Arabia, so forthcoming when Iraq had occupied Kuwait, also refused the use of their air bases. India was more helpful but that was only to put pressure on Pakistan to flush out Pakistan's own state-sponsored terrorists. Pakistan's President, General Musharraf, was eventually transparently coerced into collaborating in the military action against Taliban-controlled Afghanistan despite prospects of unrest at home as a consequence, after attempting to avert the need to do so by sending diplomatic missions to Afghanistan. The Taliban squirmed: they offered to give up bin Laden if concrete proof could be presented, they called a council of ruling clerics to decide on bin Laden's fate and ultimately politely invited him to leave (he didn't), they claimed he had left, they offered to give him up if sanctions in place against Afghanistan were raised, they massed soldiers at the borders, looted and despoiled an empty United States embassy, ostensibly ordered bin Laden out of the country. United States and British soldiers started flying in towards the war zone. The official United States stance appeared to go down well at home: Bush's popularity ratings soared; Stars and Stripes banner companies could hardly keep up with the demand. Before the end of September 2001 these war preparations had taken shape.

This was the messy and confusing picture of events in that month as gleaned from the mass media.

The messiness and confusion in this picture emerged from an uncertainty of objectives. A 'war against international terrorism' could be coherently understood as a war against an abstraction – one that had manifested itself in the happening world *as an abstraction* with such frightening consequences – that no political state could officially have any objection to fighting. The uncertainties of the source and intent of the events of 11 September were such that an aura of abstraction continued to surround the perpetrators of that attack (despite the certainty that it was bin Laden and his network); it still seemed like an act of exemplary terrorist destruction that transcended any context – the manifestation of *pure terrorism*. As such, this particular act of terrorism and other acts of terrorism seemed somehow to merge into each other, merge into the abstractness of unpredictable political terror, and most political states could accept the imperative of having to fight terrorism. India, for example, has had a persistent problem with terrorist violence (often arising from a range of secession movements in different internal territories, but also from terrorists trained and equipped in Pakistan) and could easily sympathise with greater and more coordinated international action against terrorism. The situation was not dissimilar for a large number of other countries that have experienced terrorist politics at a local level or at the instigation of their neighbours. A war against an abstraction that seems to include different experiences and tangible effects and contexts is one that causes little demur. This is a war that can be easily condoned because of its very fuzziness, because it is not clear what such a war consists in – what its means are, what exactly the specific targets are, etc. In a sense such a war is glibly accepted largely because one cannot possibly be sure in what sense this is a war; a war against an abstraction has all the metaphoric power and yet all the sense of underlying security that a loose use of the word 'war' with regard to abstractions (such as 'war against crime', 'war on unemployment', 'information war', 'gender war', etc.) has instilled in a period of relative stability.

The problem here is that for the United States, as was amply clear, the 'war against international terrorism' was not actually going to be a war against an abstraction; it soon got translated into a more conventional military affair, directed from one political state (the United States) against an international agent (Islamic fundamentalist terrorist groups) and more crucially, and in keeping with conventional notions of war, against another political state (Taliban-ruled Afghanistan), possibly even against a *number* of other political states (all those who 'harbour terrorists'). Collaborating with this was a somewhat different affair from collaborating with a broad war against an abstract 'international terrorism'. This disturbed a whole series of unilateral and multilateral agreements and understandings (overt and tacit) that existed between specific states, and a whole series of relationships that existed in the civil and cultural spheres that political states have to be sensitive to. That the United States's 'war against international terrorism' was also a conventional military affair, of course, was no surprise: that this was bound to be so was actually evident almost as soon as it was announced. But the double play on the word 'war', against an abstraction and the conventional military war, was enough for confusion to ensue. The first had to be supported, and was conceptually easy to declare support for. The second was a more complicated and practical affair, and not so easy to collaborate in unconditionally. The United States was undoubtedly aware that the lure of the first sense of war had to be maintained so that the agreements secured on its basis could be used to effect for the second sense of war that she actually had in mind. But the overall confusion was unavoidable: *two distinct kinds of war with distinct implications (one which few political states could help supporting unconditionally and another which few political states could afford to support unconditionally) were being mixed up and played off against each other.*

This observation leads to a series of questions. To what extent can a 'war against international terrorism' in abstract be equated with war as military action against a specific terrorist group or specific terrorist groups espousing a certain ideology and those that harbour them? Is there any conceptual equivalence between these two kinds of war? Further, what are the means that may conceivably be used to conduct these two kinds of war? And to what extent may they be thought of as complementing/supporting each other and to what extent as contradicting each other? To be able to answer these questions some clarification of terms is needed.

After the events of 11 September several media commentators asserted that the use of the word 'war' in 'war against international terrorism' had been ill advised. Several distinct arguments were offered to make this point. Some felt that the notion of a 'war against international terrorism' where 'international terrorism' is given as an abstraction – *all* terrorist (however defined) activity of whatever description and wherever – is meaningless. There is no realistic sense in which a war can be fought against such an amorphous and diverse entity. Others argued that declaring 'war against international terrorism' actually accords a sort of legitimacy to terrorism. There are two presumptions at work in this kind of argument. One, that in different ways war involves certain notions of legitimacy (war is fought with certain rules, war is fought by those who legitimately represent a particular alignment, a state of war has to be formally declared and understood to have been declared, war can be fought with some sense of legitimately utilitarian interest, etc.). These notions are embedded not just within a common-sense under-standing of war, but have been the matter of much systematic academic enquiry, and I will be touching on academic reflections in this area soon. Two, that perpetrators of terrorism cannot be regarded as in any sense legitimate: that any act of terrorism is by definition illegal and therefore criminal, and (this is distinct) that anyone who has to resort to violence for political purposes must be irrational. Even if, as a generalisation, this might seem suspect, in the case of the events of 11 September (where the motivations for the attack were unclear and the scale of the attack seemed incom-prehensible and beyond any utilitarian calculation) this had an air of truth about it. Others felt that the phrase 'war against inter-national terrorism' was effectively a blurring of distinctions which might effectively lead to reprisals against those who were uncon-nected with the terrorist attacks of 11 September, and may force alignments between such and the specific terrorist group/groups that were responsible for these particular attacks as a matter of pragmatism even when the former are ideologically separate from, perhaps even opposed to, the latter.

Essentially these arguments tried to come to terms with the two senses of war that were (deliberately) mixed up in the aftermath of 11 September by attempting to work out what is the relationship between warfare in general and terrorist activity in general. In attempting this they were guided by the conviction that warfare and terrorist activity should be strongly distinguished. The distinction was made by drawing upon the apparently common-sense and widely prevalent notion of warfare as military conflict at the behest of recognisable political agents – which was qualified by the idea that warfare is material (no place for abstractions), warfare follows certain rules of engagement, warfare is precisely located as occurring between adversaries whose positions are clear and identifiable. The above arguments therefore tended to be dismissive of the conceptual and pragmatic nuances of a 'war against international terrorism' by asserting that terrorist activity should not be given any space within warfare, that terrorist activity and warfare exist at different conceptual levels. Specific terrorist acts can and should lead to specific retaliations, but drawing warfare and terrorist activity

together in a general manner ('war against international terrorism')
is not acceptable. And yet, even at a common-sense level and even
with the restrictive idea of a military conflict at the behest of identifiable political agents in mind, those presumed qualifications about
warfare hold little water. Each of those qualifications can be
countered by equally commonsensical and equally widely prevalent
wisdom. It is undeniable that military conflict is itself usually as
much about abstractions as about material armed encounters:
warfare is not just conducted on a battlefield but on the home front
too, and by propaganda and diplomacy as much as with weapons,
and often for or against vast abstractions like nationality or religion
or political ideology. Warfare has seldom followed rules of
engagement: it is to be hoped that those who engage in warfare
would follow such rules, which are often laid out at length, but in
practice they seldom do (historical precedents of broken rules in war
are legion). Warfare almost inevitably draws in those who should
not be involved: each major military conflict has resulted in
enormous civilian casualties, what defines a combatant and what
doesn't is usually very far from clear, and no amount of technological sophistication can ensure that the adversaries engaged in war
are clearly located and precisely identified. It seems quite difficult
after all to make a sufficiently strong distinction between warfare
and terrorist activity with common sense presumptions.

   That the above-mentioned arguments against the United States's
vaunted 'war against international terrorism' proved to be
inadequate is because prevailing conceptualisations of warfare, it
seems to me, suffer from a blind spot. This is not confined to the
kind of common-sense and widely prevalent presumptions that I
have mentioned so far; indeed even quite rigorous and conceptually
sophisticated apprehensions of warfare seem to suffer from this blind
spot too. In fact, such rigorous and sophisticated apprehensions of
warfare do not help clear things up particularly regarding the distinction or lack thereof between warfare and terrorist activity. Most
investigations of the theory and practice of war focus on two broad
areas: the *procedure* of war (causes, strategies, technologies,
economics, alliances, outcomes, etc.), and the *ethics* of war
(addressing such questions as whether and under what circumstances can warfare be justified, given that a state of war exists what
sort of conduct can be considered legitimate and vice versa, what are
the alternatives to warfare and what are the relative merits or
otherwise of these with relation to war, etc.). These two areas are

obviously interrelated: for instance, the causes can arise from differing perceptions of who is justified; strategies could depend on what is considered to be legitimate conduct; the scope and definition of legitimate conduct may be affected by technological innovation and capability; and so on. Schematically speaking, the modes of approach that usually pertain to the two areas are somewhat different. The area of procedure is usually approached, and principles regarding procedure arrived at, in an inductive fashion – by contemplating historical evidence and taking into account relevant empirical factors. The area of ethics in war and ethical principles relevant to warfare is usually discussed in a deductive fashion – by starting with certain ethical first principles and seeing how these might apply to certain actual or hypothetical situations, or by starting with such situations and trying to discern what can reasonably be inferred for the actors involved in those situations, or a combination of both of these. Both these kinds of approach, and consequently both areas, are subject to certain difficulties that lead to divergent and sometimes contradictory inferences/conclusions. Apropos procedure: the range of historical evidence and contexts is so diverse that unambiguous procedural principles are quite difficult to arrive at, and the relevant empirical factors (types of political and ideological alignments, relevant technologies, etc.) change so rapidly – and often in such unpredictable ways – that existing procedural principles have to be constantly reconsidered and modified or abandoned. Apropos ethics: both first-principle-based arguments, and hypothetical- or actual-situation-based arguments, are amenable to a range of different approaches. Ethical considerations of war starting from first principles vary largely between absolutist (for example, that any loss of human life is unacceptable whatever the reason, or that certain kinds of collective values must be defended at all cost) and consequentialist (that warfare may or may not be justified according to the likelihood of its being able to bring about a desirable political or social change, an ideal state of affairs). In absolutist arguments the first principles are given and need to be defended, and in consequentialist arguments the desirability of the end (which needs to be determined for specific contexts and situations) acts as a first principle. Ethical considerations of war starting from actual or hypothetical situations generally assume that the agents involved in warfare are value free (there are two actors in conflict irrespective of who is justified and who isn't, and the end has to be victory for one or the other irrespective of which party is considered more worthy) and focus on the condition of the conflict and the assumption of value-free opponents. Such arguments from actual or hypothetical situations naturally depend on utilitarian considerations, and try to prescribe symmetries that would make the adversaries in question fairly matched and also to prescribe the constraints on means at their disposal that would make the victory of one or the other possible and justifiable. Such an effort is bound to be problematised by the obvious paradox of having to find balance and the possibility of victory in the same argument, by the vagaries of what precisely defines the adversaries as such (who are combatants, who are non-combatants, and who is initiating action and who being used in an instrumentalist fashion, and who is simply passive), by some doubts about what could be said to constitute victory, and by the difficulties of maintaining the notion of value-free opponents consistently for most hypothetical and almost all actual situations. An interesting combination of the two kinds of ethical arguments outlined here (starting from first principle, starting from actual or hypothetical situations) is found in the just war tradition which draws upon St Augustine's strictures about what makes a war just (*jus ad bellum*) and how a war may be conducted in a just fashion (*jus in bello*). This is afflicted with a range of divergences and uncertainties that are of the sort outlined above for the two kinds of ethical arguments.

This thumbnail sketch of the relatively rigorous and well-considered apprehensions of warfare makes it clear that this is an area which is characterised by divergent and often contradictory conclusions and a general fuzziness of description, and that such apprehensions are unlikely to clarify the distinction or lack thereof between warfare and terrorist activity. It seems to me that some progress may however be made if a finger can be put on the blind spot (that I have mentioned already) that usually slips through such considerations of war procedure and ethics. Before getting down to clarifying what exactly that blind spot is, it is worth considering briefly how such rigorous and conceptually sophisticated arguments have been applied to terrorist activity – especially 'international terrorism' – as distinct from conventional warfare.

Consequentialist arguments have often been used to justify warfare, such that it includes other kinds of political violence that may be identified with what is now thought of as 'insurgent terrorism'. The realisation of a socialist state motivated the reflections on the use of political violence and warfare in the widest sense for V.I. Lenin, Mao Zedong, Ernesto Che Guevara and Carlos Marighella, for instance,[1] and the realisation of a decolonised state before that of a socialist state had led to considerations of the legitimacy and illegitimacy of political violence in different forms by Frantz Fanon, Aimé Césare and numerous other theorists and activists in colonised countries.[2] Infringement of certain first principles (the limits of infringement of the human dignity of the proletariat), and utilitarian considerations (the only way to effectively express a position) formed the backbone of Georges Sorel's apology for political violence, and Jean-Paul Sartre's perception of the violence that oppression breeds and how that could be channelled in emancipatory directions.[3] Sorel's kind of violence does not extend to the scale or coordination of military conflict (is not warfare in that conventional sense then) but again may include such acts as may now be thought of as 'insurgent terrorism'. The loose use of 'insurgent terrorism' to cover these conceptualisations and enactments of political violence is undoubtedly a matter of ideological location. From the ideological perspective of the above-mentioned theorists/activists the perpetrators of such political violence hold the just position, and could be regarded as defending themselves (conducting a 'counterterrorist offensive', in modern jargon) against the terrorism of the state. 'State terrorism' is an important issue that I will necessarily touch on in the context of the events of 11 September in due course (Chapter 5). From the generally conservative ideological perspective of the political state against which such political violence may be directed, the perpetrators of such acts of violence are 'insurgent terrorists'. Despite the ambiguity of having relativistic perspectives of what is 'terrorism' and what is 'counterterrorism', or what is terrorist activity and what is warfare, this contained form of political violence allows for a general overall clarity. It is on the whole clear which side of the ideological fence the parties in question are on, it is understood that terms are dependent on that location and that though terrorism may be theorised with a wide – ostensibly universal – ideological concern it is essentially a phenomenon *within* (confined to the precincts of a nation or society, or an area under state jurisdiction). This general clarity started getting blurred in the latter part of the Cold War (after the nineteen-sixties) with the conceptualisation of a modern 'international terrorism' which, while still being ideologically partisan, started carrying some sense of an ideologically devoid and irresponsible political violence from irrational formations with random targets, directed against humanity and humaneness per se (on an indistinguishably international scale). Moreover, this 'international terrorism' began to be understood as being directed against humanity from *without* (always from outside the boundaries of 'our nation', 'our society', 'our country', 'our people', etc., from 'foreign sources', from 'antisocial elements'). This connotation of 'international terrorism' could be distinguished from the 'insurgent terrorism' of the IRA or ETA. The term nevertheless continued to be ideologically partisan in that in the United States and Western Europe 'international terrorism' was largely seen as something that was initiated and supported by communists, and in the Soviet Union and Eastern Europe and other communist countries it was seen as being sponsored predominantly by capitalists. That ideologically devoid character that had touched the term 'international terrorism' (despite its being ideologically loaded) in the course of the Cold War, became the predominant sense of 'international terrorism' after the Cold War: now it *definitively* became ideologically devoid and irresponsible political violence from irrational formations, directed against all humanity. This is, of course, not really an ideologically nonpartisan or universal position, but is often regarded as being so (I don't elaborate on this here since that would only elongate this digression). What is pertinent to this study, written in the context of the terrorist attacks of 11 September, is how the rigorous and theoretically sophisticated apprehensions of warfare outlined above attach to this particular sense of 'international terrorism' and terrorist activity.

A survey of literature by theorists who have carried out such rigorous and sophisticated analyses of warfare shows that they don't deal particularly well with terrorist activity – especially with the special connotations of 'international terrorism' – and find it difficult to decide whether it can be accommodated in any way within their perspectives of warfare (as definitively and convincingly outside the scope of warfare, or as within the scope of warfare under certain or perhaps even all circumstances).[4] An instinctive desire to make a strong distinction between warfare and terrorist activity appears to predominate, but often this is not substantiated by philosophically adequate arguments. From a procedural perspective it is undeniable that terrorist activity could be regarded as a specific sort of warfare or a subset within a larger conflict that is (conventionally) warfare, which involves a particular apprehension of causes (even if this apprehension is considered irrational it could still be a cause), follows certain strategies (indirect rather than direct), uses available technologies, has its own (perhaps covert) economic calculations and networks, and has almost indistinguishable effects from those of warfare (the use of destructive force to outmanoeuvre or destabilise an opponent, a psychological effect of terror and insecurity amongst those who support an opponent). That terrorist activity could be regarded as a particular procedural facet of warfare seems nevertheless to militate against the rigorous theorist's instincts, and strong distinctions between warfare and terrorist activity (especially under 'international terrorism') are therefore drawn on ethical grounds. Ethical arguments drawn from absolutist first principles could either reject or accept warfare as well as terrorist activity on the same grounds. An absolute principle cannot be compromised at any cost, so a distinction between warfare and terrorist activity is immaterial unless it can be shown that terrorist activity compromises such a principle while warfare doesn't, or vice versa. It is very difficult indeed to find a persuasive absolute first principle that can be used to make such a distinction between warfare and terrorist activity – and absolute first principles have naturally almost never been called upon to make such a distinction. Consequentialist arguments provide the bulk of attempts at making a clear distinction between warfare and terrorism. Briefly, the argument is that terrorism in general, and especially with the connotations now attached to 'international terrorism', is unlikely to effect any hoped for outcome whereas warfare would decide the issue in contention one way or another. Partly this is attributed to the notion that since terrorist activity (especially as 'international terrorism') depends single-mindedly on fear and coercion it is unlikely to convince anyone that the outcome that terrorists seek can be better than the one that exists, and resistance to it is likely to be stiff; whereas warfare is usually conducted between parties that can call upon wider authority and solidarity (whether deserved or not) that is at least recognised and agreed upon in advance. This however is far from being a sound argument: there is no way of validating the claim that parties engaged in warfare are not single-mindedly coercive; and there is no way of arguing that even if terrorist activity is single-mindedly coercive it could not achieve, for its purposes, a sufficient following (the rationale of stable coexistence can obviously be superseded by factors such as faith or dogmatism or some notion of kinship). Generally, therefore, consequentialists take the utilitarian path and assume methodological arguments more familiar to procedural considerations of warfare. It may be asserted in this strain that historical precedent shows that what is considered to be terrorist activity has seldom been successful, whereas what is thought of as warfare usually reaches a result which is positive or negative for one of the warring parties. If that is accepted then it is evident that there are utilitarian grounds for engaging in what is clearly understood to be warfare, but none in what is perceived as terrorist activity. The problem here is that historical precedent shows no such thing: Edward Hyams, for instance, argued in 1975 that historical precedent shows how effective terrorism can be and that to think otherwise is no more than a wishful orthodoxy.[5] The various grounds on which specific consequentialist arguments about terrorism have been flawed have been discussed usefully by Burleigh Taylor Wilkins.[6] This leaves us with the just war tradition, according to which it is likely that what is now understood as 'international terrorism' would be condemned as a priori unjust, whereas clearly it assumes that under certain conditions warfare can be just. However, there always remains the possibility that 'international terrorism' can be understood as unjust warfare – so warfare nevertheless; and there remains the distinct possibility that no war in practice has ever been just in the strictly conceptual sense (i.e. in having followed the prescriptions of justness that are laid down by or inferred from the just war tradition).

What emerges from that rather lengthy perambulation on apparently rigorous and conceptually sophisticated apprehensions of warfare (necessary, I felt, to put the bulk of the existing scholarship and thinking on warfare and terrorism into perspective) is that, despite a strong predisposition to make a distinction between warfare and terrorist activity, no such sound distinction has been or can be made. On the whole, this complex of conceptualisations of warfare and terrorist activity could have been circumvented if – coming back to this now – that blind spot I mentioned earlier hadn't had such a hold on most serious engagements with the theory and practice of war.

The approaches to warfare discussed above hope to understand *what war is* by examining the procedure and ethics of war. And yet unless there is a prior understanding of *what war is* it is not possible to discuss the procedure and ethics that characterise it. It is generally assumed in approaches such as those discussed that we all more or less know *what war is* already; these approaches then proceed to tell us *what war is* by analysing the procedural characteristics and ethical issues that are recognisably attached to what we already *recognise as and understand to be war*; and finally they end up by suggesting that the analysis has actually revealed *what war is*. This is a circular argument in that it depends on our already knowing *what war is*, providing a discussion on the basis of that and finally coming to the conclusion that somehow this discussion has revealed to us *what war is*. What slips through is precisely that which is assumed to begin with and understood as revealed at the end: *what is war?* Recent discussions of warfare do not seem to feel that that question needs to be addressed in a headlong fashion: they start with the attitude that this is known already and can be discussed, and end with the conviction that it has been discussed and is therefore known now. But the question does need to be addressed because in fact neither a discussion of procedural considerations nor of relevant ethical issues quite tell us *what war is*. If we know the answer to that we can always discuss meaningfully the numerous – indeed innumerable – procedural considerations that attach to warfare, and recognise yet others as being relevant, even though we hadn't thought of them before, on the basis of that answer. If we expect to find the answer by charting out and examining the numerous procedural considerations that are usually thought of as pertinent to warfare, we are likely to artificially limit the scope of *what war is* to what we have examined, and to miss out many procedural considerations that we didn't recognise as relevant but which are in fact so. Nor is a discussion of ethical issues apropos warfare likely to tell us *what war is*: ethical issues in this case involve clarifications and qualifications *within what war is* and therefore do not quite tell us *what war is* (on the contrary they assume that as a whole and in essence this is known, but in specific details and contexts could be clarified or qualified). So *what war is* usually keeps slipping through ethical discussions that do not address that question directly: that ethical arguments prefer to clarify what consequences warfare is undertaken for does not mean that war can be understood solely in terms of the consequences it is undertaken for; that ethical arguments try to validate certain situations and agreements in warfare does not mean that war cannot be fought in terms which cannot be so validated and agreed upon; that ethical considerations declare certain practices to be legitimate or just in warfare does not mean that illegitimate or unjust warfare is not war; and so on. What slips through is that blind spot: *what is war?*

To get an answer, it seems, we need to go back to the first few pages of Carl von Clausewitz's classic *On War* – as scholars repeatedly do whenever they momentarily become aware of this question. Their attention is usually drawn to what looks like the closest thing to a definition of war:

> War is nothing but a duel on a larger scale. Countless duels go to make up war, but a picture of it as a whole can be formed by imagining a pair of wrestlers. Each tries through physical force to compel the other to do his will; his *immediate* aim is to *throw* his opponent in order to make him incapable of further resistance.
> *War is thus an act of force to compel our enemy to do our will.*[7]

After noting this it seems to be customary in scholarly works to be struck by the sense of absolute war or uncompromising opposition, a continuing no-holds-barred process that spirals out in different ways (which Clausewitz carefully charts out and reflects on) toward victory/defeat/truce/incompleteness and thereafter.[8] However the usual preoccupation with this aspect of Clausewitz's theorisation seems to me to be a distraction from the definitive element within that statement. The sense of absolute opposition in Clausewitz's understanding of war is striking mainly because it seems to be revealing and yet to be elusive at the same time; the effect is to distract from the nuances and general applicability of the definition. It is the case though that the germ of a quite inclusive and obvious definition of war does lie within that statement. Incidentally, one may also be struck by the similarity of the (brief) process through which Clausewitz approaches war as a whole to the (lengthy) process through which Sartre engages with the working of pure dialectics – totalised conflict-in-itself – from an existentialist point of view. In the second volume of *The Critique of Dialectical Reason* Sartre tries to conceive of this by starting with a philosophical ploy used effectively and often by him: the visualisation of a concrete and familiar image. This allows him both to slowly work out the too obvious and therefore invisible associations that the image arouses (thereby analysing the broader significances of that image), and to effectively strip away the association to give the image a stark essential – or rather existential – significance. In trying to work out the existential centrality of dialectics as conflict-in-itself, Sartre starts with a brilliant analysis of the image of a boxing match as exemplifying individuated conflict (not unlike Clausewitz's duellists or wrestlers) and builds up from there to the conflict of pledged groups or social subgroups (he doesn't go as far as war, but then he was concerned with the state of society as a whole and not the particular condition of war).[9] I do not mention Sartre here in a spirit of pedantry: his extensive application of this philosophical method throws a vivid light on Clausewitz's brief but to-the-point statement. The point of the statement is not to lead on to other things (causes, strategies, means, outcomes, legitimacy, purposes, etc.) but to provide – as Sartre does when he gradually strips his images of their associations and comes to an existential core of the matter under consideration – the focus of a definition of war, an answer to *what is war*: *war is defined at the initial point when two large-scale alignments (however or in whatever terms 'large' may be understood, certainly larger than individual or even a few individuals) actively engage with each other with the definite intention of overcoming or subduing the other by force.* That is the core of the matter, all the other considerations (causes, strategies, means, outcomes, legitimacy, purposes, etc.) are ancillary to or corollaries of that. And yet, the import of Clausewitz's statement, even if seen thus, is not complete; Clausewitz makes a crucial qualification, which has to be included within that statement, soon afterwards:

> War, however, is not the action of a living force upon a lifeless mass (total unresistance would be no war at all) but always the collision of two living forces. The ultimate aim of waging war, as formulated here, must be taken as applying to both sides.[10]

That has to be included in the above definition. A war wouldn't be a war unless the active intention to overcome the other is entertained by both sides. This in turn suggests that at the initial point when two parties engage with each other as described above there must be some sense of equivalence which would give their forceful engagement and intention the character of war. This equivalence need not be a matter of strength or weakness: obviously two nations can engage in warfare with each other even if the forces of one are immensely better armed and trained than those of the other. What operates here is the principle of equivalence in terms of the sovereignty of nations: that principle is enough to ensure that any conflict between nations which expresses the will of each nation to overcome the other (whether aggressively or defensively) is war. This equivalence could also be in terms of strategy: so, for example, warfare can be conducted between a revolutionary alignment and a repressive political state by the former's gaining equivalence to the latter's superior military capabilities by using guerrilla tactics. Equivalence could also perhaps be a matter of determination and popular support between otherwise unevenly matched opponents. By equivalence here, in fact, I gesture towards that which allows two warring sides to begin their engagement with each other with what Clausewitz calls 'living force'. Otherwise there would be defeat before war, like a massacre or an occupation without repercussions. So here's a slightly modified, and it seems to me serviceable, answer to that question, *what is war? – war is defined at the initial point when two large-scale alignments (however or in whatever terms 'large' may be understood, certainly 'large' in terms of involving and affecting more than an individual or even a few individuals), which are characterised by some principle of equivalence, actively engage with each other, each with the definite intention of overcoming or subduing the other by force.*

The principle of equivalence that is included in the definition given above is gestured towards in interesting though not always successful ways in Quincy Wright's monumental *A Study of War* (1942). Wright's attempts at defining war in fact always circle around the notion of equivalence. At the beginning of his study he gives a broad definition of war: '[...] war is a *violent contact of distant* but *similar* entities',[11] and immediately proceeds to narrow this down to fit the concerns of contemporary warfare: 'For this purpose war will be considered the *legal condition* which *equally* permits two or more *hostile groups* to carry on a *conflict* by *armed* force.'[12] The use of the words 'similar' and 'equally' in the two definitions respectively seem to me to take account of what I have called a principle of equivalence here. But this is somewhat complicated by the emphasis on *legal* perception and sanction ('permits'), which is actually emphasised when he tries to draw the relationship between the terms of the broader and the narrower definitions, and especially of the two terms that concern us here:

> Instead of 'similar' entities, implying resemblance in such observable qualities as size, structure and appearance, the warring entities are said to have equality under law. This suggests that in spite of their hostility they are members of a higher group which originates this law.[13]

The emphasis on legal perception and sanction restricts the connotations of the broader 'similar' so much, conflates the legal-ethical with the procedural to such a degree, that it becomes materially useless. It has to be assumed, if one is to follow Wright, that in a contemporary situation a conflict cannot be considered a war unless it has some sort of legal sanction – that war is a legal term. This leads to the rather absurd position that even if two parties regard themselves as being engaged in a war with large-scale effects, and have some sort of strategic equivalence, the conflict may from that narrowly legal point of view not be regarded as war (and not be *permitted* – though what may that mean?) if one or even both the parties do not subscribe to the law, do not own allegiance to that 'higher group which originates the law'. Wright is more successful when he comes back to defining war later in his book, with a view to discerning what war might mean to either of the warring parties and what the observable effects might consist in – indeed this later definition is quite useful in giving substance to the principle of equivalence:

> War may [...] be regarded from the standpoint of each belligerent as an extreme intensification of military activity, psychological tension, legal power, and social integration – an intensification which is not likely to result unless the enemy is approximately equal in material power. From the standpoint of all belligerents war may be considered a simultaneous conflict of armed forces, popular feelings, jural dogmas, and national cultures so nearly equal as to lead to an extreme intensification of each.[14]

While this is more successful as an understanding of equivalence, it is still a limited understanding – it is *one* sort of understanding that focuses on the equality in 'material power'. It leaves no space, for instance, for equivalence in terms of strategic manoeuvres or sheer determination or will (what Clausewitz more aptly calls 'life'), even where the armed forces, the relevant jural dogma or the national cultures may be asymmetrical or imbalanced in different ways.

At any rate, with the definition stated in italics above in hand I can return to the relationship of terrorism to warfare.

Terrorist activity, including that with the particular connotations of 'international terrorism', *is* an aspect of warfare or a kind of warfare or a part of warfare – is, at any rate, within the precincts of war. It fulfils all the conditions that define war. There are two large-scale alignments: not necessarily large-scale in the case of both alignments, but certainly one of them would be large in numerical terms. A terrorist organisation may have no more than a few members. In principle a terrorist act may also be perpetrated by an individual and still be regarded as terrorist insofar as it is perpetrated and/or understood to be perpetrated for political ends. Terrorist acts perpetrated by a numerically small group would nevertheless be regarded as large-scale because their target would be so: the undermining of an existing social organisation, the defiance of a political state and its machinery, inspiring the feeling of insecurity amongst a populace or section of a populace. Any terrorist activity is an act of force (however crude or sophisticated it might be) with a view to asserting a political position of some sort (however just or unjust) and subverting another established one (again however just or unjust) – intentionally seeking the downfall of an alignment that espouses a different position (irrespective of the chances of success). The principle of initial equivalence is maintained on strategic grounds. This matter of equivalence on strategic grounds is worth teasing out a bit further – it shows how far thinking about terrorism is geared towards *internal* or 'insurgent terrorism', and the fact that this is still so may confuse our grasp of 'international terrorism'.

Essentially, those undertaking terrorist activity attempt to find equivalence with a larger enemy (usually a political state – or range of political states – that naturally has at its disposal all the means that are normally understood to give a state its monopoly on force within an area under its jurisdiction) by assuming a method of warfare whereby they are exposed as little as possible for the enemy to take action against them. The method depends on surprise, on the perpetrators being able to conceal themselves or hide among a population, and on their being able to cause such damage that a psychological effect is produced (of uncertainty, or terror) and attention is drawn to the acts (thereby undermining the authority of the enemy, and perhaps achieving publicity for the terrorist's perspective). In attempting to find equivalence through this strategy, terrorist activity is in fact formally similar to the extensively theorised and examined area of guerrilla warfare. As Everett L. Wheeler observes in 'Terrorism and Military Theory' (1991): 'Just as in guerrilla warfare, the pinpricks of terrorism permit a numerically or technologically weaker party to annoy and embarrass a superior force without the face-to-face confrontation in which the superior party can exert its strength.'[15] However, this is likely to remind those informed of these matters that many experts are convinced that there are significant differences between terrorist activity and guerrilla warfare. Walter Laqueur asserts that though some parties tend to obfuscate the distinction between guerrilla warfare and terrorist activity (mainly because the former appears to have more positive connotations and the latter is regarded as a pejorative term, and it is therefore in the interest of those involved in terrorist activity to present themselves as guerrilla), a clear distinction should be maintained – though he doesn't actually explain what the distinction is.[16] Ariel Merari in 'Terrorism as a Strategy of Insurgency' (1993), where he examines 'terrorism as a mode of struggle rather than a social or political aberration',[17] takes it on himself to explain the difference at some length:

> As strategies of insurgency [...] terrorism and guerrilla are quite distinct. The most important difference is that unlike terrorism, guerrilla tries to establish physical control of a territory. This control is often partial. [...] The need to dominate territory is a key element in insurgent guerrilla strategy. The territory under the guerrilla's control provides the human reservoir for recruitment, a logistical base and – most importantly – the ground and infrastructure for establishing a regular army.[18]

He goes on to enumerate other lesser, but still material, differences: guerrillas use platoon- or company-sized units in their actions while terrorists use smaller units; guerrillas use traditional military-style weapons while terrorists usually innovate with bombs and less conventional weapons; guerrillas often wear uniforms and terrorists do not; guerrillas, like the military, adhere to certain rules (at least in principle, even if these are flouted in practice) whereas terrorist acts are designed to express disdain for such rules and to subvert them. From these differences Merari concludes that '[...] whereas guerrilla and conventional war are two modes of warfare which are different in strategy but similar in tactics, terrorism is a unique form of struggle in both strategy and tactics'.[19] The conclusion is patently misleading: there is, as Wheeler says, marked similarity between guerrilla strategy and the strategy of terrorist activity, even though a distinction can clearly be made in terms of tactics. However, even the distinction in tactics needs to be qualified further: Merari seems to assign guerrilla warfare and terrorist activity to diametrically opposed and sharply defined tactical spaces – this suggests an either–or situation. Given however that there are strategic similarities, it is quite possible that guerrillas may resort to what may tactically be thought of as terrorist activity. The tactic of 'hit and run' that Guevara had marked out as the initial phase of guerrilla warfare[20] may well include acts which are strictly speaking within the sphere of terrorist tactics in Merari's terms (without any immediate advantage in terms of territorial control and more for creating a psychological effect, conducted in a small unit, without uniforms, with unconventional weapons, etc.). I suspect that despite his determination not to be swayed by the moral connotations of 'guerrilla' and 'terrorist', arguments such as Merari's (which seek to find clear distinctions between the two) are in fact often insidiously guided by the moral emphases of these terms.

What is interesting however is not the arguments about the distinction between terrorism and guerrilla warfare in themselves but the inadequacy of these arguments when we come to the prevailing connotations of 'international terrorism'. Such arguments have been predicated on terrorist activity *within*, on what passes for 'insurgent terrorism'. The main distinction (quoted above) that Merari depends on, territorial control, shows how indelibly these arguments are allied to 'insurgent terrorism' and how redundant they have now become in the face of 'international terrorism'. Such arguments are based on strategies of warfare *within a defined territory where the two warring parties are vying for control*. It is possible to compare and contrast recognised forms of warfare (guerrilla or conventional) and 'insurgent terrorism' (guerrilla or not) where both have the immediate common denominator of being conducted within a discrete territory. But a war between parties *across* territorial boundaries is a different matter: i.e. a war between two alignments that is not to determine direct control of a discrete territory but to determine the strength of ideological control in a wider sense (say, in terms of trying to institute a particular form of economic and administrative organisation across a range of initially unidentified nations, or of clarifying these with regard to a third and apparently uninvolved party, or of being in a position to influence people of different denominations generally by controlling certain means of influence). Such wars across territorial boundaries could of course be fought in terms of conventional military tactics and strategies – as, for example, the French and the British fought a series of wars to determine prerogatives of colonial control of uninvolved territories in Asia and the Americas in the eighteenth century. (Convention and political exigency have now come to deny any resort to such wars for direct territorial control where those in the territory in question are not directly involved.) Warfare with international imperatives usually involves two or more political states who fight using conventional military tactics and strategies, and depend on their predecided initial equivalence of representing sovereign nations. If such a war however commences between political formations that do not have such a predecided initial equivalence of principle (ideological groupings which are not territorially discrete), or between such a political grouping and a political state, then this condition of initial equivalence cannot be drawn upon. Under these circumstances equivalence would necessarily have to be sought in strategic and tactical terms, rather than in principle, if the ensuing engagement is to be understood as war. At this international scale there is actually little space for guerrilla warfare as understood by Merari since the definitive matter of territorial control is not the immediate issue of the engagement. The main instance in recent years of such political groupings going to war with political states with guerrilla tactics and strategies is the warfare that has been undertaken by certain revolutionary socialist alignments. Despite the fact that revolutionary socialist alignments owed allegiance to what they considered to be an internationally effective ideology, and often depended on solidarity with and support from an international movement, such wars were actually primarily conducted within discrete territories (for example, the successful revolutionary wars *within* Russia, Mexico, China, Cuba, etc.). Insofar as revolutionary socialism has depended on opposing state power with guerrilla tactics it has done so within a discrete territory and against the established state within that territory. But the situation which obviously obtains in the consideration of 'international terrorism', where a political grouping fights a war against another/other political state/states with no immediate objective of territorial control within a clearly defined territory, guerrilla tactics as Merari understands them are not an option. However the need to try to find initial equivalence through strategic means (which would make the war a war), as is usually involved in guerrilla warfare, is obvious. Under these circumstances it seems to me that neither conventional nor guerrilla warfare is possible: under these circumstances the only kind of warfare that is possible is that which involves terrorist strategies and tactics.

Let me emphasise again that the arguments presented in the above two paragraphs are not with regard to the moral connotations of terrorist activity as compared to those of conventional military warfare or guerrilla warfare; they are with regard to the comparative strategies and tactics involved. There is a significant conclusion to be drawn from this perspective: *the circumstances and positions from which 'international terrorism', which is a form of warfare, arises could not arise in any other form than that of terrorism – they arise because military conflict in a conventional sense cannot be engaged in with any meaningful initial equivalence and because guerrilla warfare (definitively geared towards territorial control) cannot apply.*

Having clarified to some extent the procedural considerations that attach to 'international terrorism' once it is understood as being squarely within the arena of warfare, we are left with an obvious ethical consideration. It is clear that there is a kind of strategic and tactical reasoning in the warfare that involves 'international terrorist' activity: the question is whether any, and precisely what kind of, moral opprobrium attaches to that activity, that procedure of warfare, *in itself* (without immediately having to clarify the context or causes of a particular 'international terrorist' act)? Having recognised that under certain constraints (which can be demarcated in a theoretical fashion without taking immediate recourse to specific acts, contexts and circumstances) 'international terrorism' is indisputedly a form of warfare, can we determine at the same level of abstraction whether 'international terrorism' can be unequivocally considered to be morally unacceptable or otherwise? To examine this briefly I draw upon a description of terrorist strategic logic given by Michael Walzer in *Just and Unjust Wars* (1977), which both adheres to a concept of strategic reasoning that seems to be especially close to 'international terrorist' warfare (and especially in the context of 11 September) and inspires instantaneous instinctive moral repugnance, without taking recourse to an immediate discussion of specific terrorist acts:

> The systematic terrorizing of whole populations is a strategy of both conventional and guerrilla war, and of established governments as well as radical movements. Its purpose: to destroy the morale of a nation or a class, to undercut its solidarity; its method is the random murder of innocent people. Randomness is the crucial feature of terrorist activity. If one wishes fear to spread and intensify over time, it is not desirable to kill specific people identified in some particular way with a regime, a party, or a policy. Death must come by chance to individual Frenchmen, or Germans, to Irish Protestants, or Jews, simply because they are Frenchmen or Germans, Protestants or Jews, until they feel

themselves fatally exposed and demand that their governments negotiate for their safety.

In war, terrorism is a way of avoiding engagement with the enemy army. It represents an extreme form of the strategy of the 'indirect approach.'[21]

There are some clarifications that need to be made about this quotation before undertaking an analysis of it with the above-stated questions in mind. Walzer rightly observes that the psychological effect of mass terror is one that all kinds of warfare may resort to. For our purpose it may be inferred from this that the psychological effect that terrorist activity, among other kinds of warfare, calculatedly or otherwise brings about cannot itself be the subject of a moral judgement that can attach exclusively to terrorist warfare. Walzer goes on to note that it is the *method* that is used to bring about the effect (a psychological effect) that crucially distinguishes terrorism: the method of the 'random murder of innocent people'. The emphasis of the *method* brings us within the area of the strategic and tactical in terrorism (qualified later as an 'indirect approach'), and that method is stated in terms that do imply, at least instinctively, a moral perspective (the emphasis on *randomness*, the use of the word *murder*, the characterisation of the victims as *innocent*). In Walzer's clarification of what randomness means it immediately becomes evident that what he has in mind is not *absolute* or *indiscriminate* randomness. There *are* targets that can be characterised as French, German etc. What Walzer might mean by randomness here is that such characterisation does not form adequate grounds for demarcating specificity; targets so broadly characterised cannot be considered to be properly targets at all and therefore have to be thought of as randomly affected. Alternatively, or perhaps simultaneously, Walzer might be suggesting that from the perspective of the German, French, etc. individual victims of a terrorist attack this would seem to be a random attack because such individuals might not especially define themselves as defending German, French, etc. interests or identify themselves particularly with that which the terrorists hope to overcome. Implicit in both these possibilities is the notion of innocence that Walzer adjectivally brings up. The 'innocence' of victims of terrorism has naturally been a matter for debate in theoretical discussions of terrorism.[22] Without going into the complexities of this at any length the senses in which 'innocence' may pertinently apply to Walzer's characterisation of the casualties of terrorist method could be put as follows:

1. The casualties as a whole may be considered innocent in that their targeting was not determined by any effort to sort out who amongst them actually adheres to or conforms to that which the group perpetuating the terrorist attack wishes to overcome.
2. The casualties who can be broadly characterised as French, German, etc. may be thought of as innocent in that their being French, German, etc. was not (irrespective of how they might feel about being part of that category) a matter of choice – they just happened to be such (just as some people just happen to be white or black, men or women, young or old).
3. The casualties of any terrorist attack that doesn't arise out of more specific targeting can be considered innocent in that such persons had not understood themselves as being in or had not agreed to be in a position whereby untimely loss, trauma, or death was a distinct possibility (thus distinguishing them from combatants of any description, who have to be considered as prepared for this just by being combatants in some sense).

These are the senses that attach coherently to Walzer's characterisation of the 'innocence' of victims of terrorism.

With these qualifications in mind and given Walzer's specific presentation of terrorist strategic logic and its moral implications, let's come back to the question that concerns us here. If this is understood as a particularly apt general description of the kind of 'international terrorism' (as warfare) that concerns us here, is it possible to determine without further contextualisation whether such 'international terrorism' can be considered to be unequivocally morally unacceptable in *contrast* to other kinds of warfare (conventional, guerrilla)? Even in Walzer's relatively morally loaded terms, and despite the affirmative that we might feel instinctively inclined to give this, this is actually a difficult question to answer. The answer would depend on our ability to give unequivocal answers to a few related questions:

a. Walzer does concede that all wars can strategically draw upon the usefulness of generating terror within a populace, albeit with different methods. The differences in method are presumably marked by the degree of specific and random targeting of people that is involved. If generating terror within a populace at large becomes a military strategy in a conventional or guerrilla war situation, it might well become the strategy of an army systematically to kill some civilians in a particularly ghastly fashion, or systematically to make all civilians suffer by the threat of, say, cutting food supplies (or more indirectly, imposing economic sanctions) or displacing them from their homesteads, or simply by the uncertainty of being inadvertently affected by the targeted attack of certain combatant forces (bombing strategic positions). *Is the mass terror that is generated by such targeted warfare different from that which is generated by the random attack warfare of terrorism?* [From all sorts of moral perspectives the answer to this seems to me to leave little distinction between 'international terrorism' and other kinds of warfare.]

b. *Is it pragmatically possible to conceive of any warfare where mass terror is not generated, and where some random casualties (however unwilfully this comes about) are not expected?* [*Pragmatically* I doubt it.]

c. *If* it is accepted that some people will be randomly killed or hurt in a (conventional or guerrilla) war situation, the moral distinction from Walzer's description of terrorism might have to rest on interpretation of intent: whether casualties occur inevitably, despite the best efforts being made to keep them to a minimum, or whether they occur because exactly this result was deliberately engineered. *How precisely can we distinguish between consequences that are similar even though the intentions that are claimed as causing those consequences might be quite different – even diametrically opposed?* [In this question we might be assisted by considering legal methods of distinguishing between culpable homicide and unlawful killing, for instance. Typically, legal judgement cannot be made in an ad hoc fashion and needs close consideration of specific contexts, persons, motives and outcomes. That a military unit claims that it had killed the inhabitants of a village full of innocent non-combatants because of a misunderstanding does not mean that they told the truth. The circumstances need to be examined. If the inhabitants of a village full of innocent non-combatants are killed and a terrorist group claims responsibility does this not also have to be examined with similar attention to circumstances? Assessing claims and intentions can be a tricky business and is seldom open to unambiguous general evaluative propositions.]

d. Certain kinds of utilitarian moral thinking do allow for the assessment of means in terms of ends. The strategic terrorist logic that Walzer describes, so closely allied to the current connotations of 'international terrorism', can arguably be – as I have shown – an inevitable one to obtain initial conditions of equivalence under which war could be undertaken. I think it is reasonably clear that the instinctive repugnance that we are inclined to feel at the murder of innocents draws on some such moral position as that 'innocent people shouldn't be punished (die, suffer) for something they are not responsible for' (a principle of just retribution). If taken as an absolutist principle this would render any kind of warfare unjustified. If taken in a utilitarian spirit the principle can be superseded under certain circumstances whereby a more desirable end is achieved. *Is it possible to conceive of an act of 'international terrorism' with regard to which the perpetrators may argue (on the grounds of the inevitability of the means it uses given the circumstances and the desirability of the end that it passionately espouses) that its means be considered as outweighing the principle of just retribution?* [Again, it seems to me that this question cannot be conclusively answered unless the specific circumstances of the act in question and arguments that the terrorists may offer are examined, if we wish to stay within the utilitarian framework.]

Such questions and the doubts they raise might seem perverse given our instinctive predisposition to accept conventional or guerrilla warfare easily and denounce terrorism out of hand. But these are also questions and doubts that cannot be thrown aside without discussion.

I chose Walzer's morally loaded description of a strategic terrorist logic because this logic seemed to me to be strategically coherent and yet apparently most easily condemnable in moral terms. It is an apprehension of terrorism that coheres with the above-discussed understanding of terrorism as war, and that simultaneously conveys a sense of moral outrage, and therefore seemed ideal for investigating whether the strategic logic and moral outrage were necessarily linked. It is of course clear that terrorist strategy could be expressed in more neutral ways or understood in ways such that its moral connotations are not immediately evident. But Walzer's description seems to ensure that *at least for this description* the strategic logic and the moral outrage would be necessarily linked. Since Walzer's description of terrorism does not attempt to immediately fix specific circumstances and contexts, it could be surmised that such moral outrage as could be inferred would also not need to be conditional on specific circumstances and contexts – i.e. could therefore be inferred at a level of generality that is consistent with observations made so far in this chapter. What I feel the four questions delineated above do show is that in fact it is quite difficult to chart out un-equivocal and unambiguous reasons for condemning terrorism even as Walzer describes it, *as contrasted* with conventional and guerrilla warfare, without taking into consideration more specific contexts and circumstances – and especially so as to allow a moral distinction to be made with other kinds of warfare. Let me emphasise that *I am not saying that I do not think that such moral distinctions can be made. I am saying that such moral distinctions cannot be made at this level of generality – it is extremely difficult to answer those questions on the basis of what Walzer presents as terrorism and determine clearly why terrorism is morally unacceptable; such moral distinctions can undoubtedly be made if more information is given about specific circumstances and contexts in which terrorist acts occur.* There are in fact two ways in which we could begin to consider whether those questions can be given clear answers. One, we could draw upon specific historical precedents wherein acts which match Walzer's description have taken place and examine them in the light of those questions. Two, we could draw a typology of different kinds of terrorist acts that as a whole fit Walzer's description (i.e. hypothesise a few characteristics which allow us to differentiate kinds of terrorist acts which otherwise pertain to Walzer's description), and then try to determine whether that allows clearer answers to those questions to emerge. Though academic rigour may recommend the adoption of one or both of these at this point, I feel that neither is actually necessary for this particular study.

Let me bring this study back more firmly to its principal concern: the understanding of 'international terrorism' in the wake of the terrorist attacks in the United States on 11 September 2001. All the above theoretical considerations have been outlined and enumerated with the aim of trying to come to grips with 'inter-national terrorism' as a result of these particular events. I do not need to go through the actual or hypothetical specific circumstances and contexts that would allow me to chart out the moral conditions which differentiate terrorism (as Walzer describes it) from other kinds of war, because I have predetermined one particular context and set of circumstances as the main focus here. Despite the gaps and lacunae that remain in the above theoretical discussion (undoubtedly matter for many theses and elaborations), I think enough of a sense of a theoretical background and of the pertinent issues has been conveyed to concentrate on the main focus. The main focus, at the point at which I left it at the beginning of this chapter, was the two senses of war that emerged in response to the events of 11 September: 'war against international terrorism' in abstract; war as military action against specific terrorist groups (first bin Laden and al-Quaeda) and the countries that gave such groups refuge (Taliban-controlled Afghanistan).

Let me briefly summarise the events of 11 September in the light of the above theoretical observations. War was effectively declared and commenced on 11 September 2001. A terrorist strike of large magnitude, with an extraordinary scale of casualties, could not be mistaken as being other than an act of war – at least by effect, if not by the constituency of the enemy, this was large enough to be brought immediately under the aegis of warfare. Just by the scale of casualties this could not be construed simply as a criminal act, even by those who have habitually (and often controversially) so construed smaller-scale terrorist activity. The scale of casualties ensured that this couldn't be responded to within the area of policing alone. However, one characteristic of an act of war was missing: the enemy didn't announce its intention and didn't claim responsibility. In this case, however, that simply underlined that a state of war had been declared and had commenced with the attacks. It was clear that in the very perpetration of these attacks the enemy had established equivalence with the very considerable state power of the United States. The targets were chosen – especially the Pentagon – as an announcement of that equivalence. Indications that the nation was terrorised and holding her breath in suspense demonstrated that the announcement of equivalence had been received: in the following months every suspicious death, every unpredictable act of violence in the United States – a mad man trying to kill a bus driver, another deranged person trying to storm the cockpit of an aeroplane – was immediately assumed to be another terrorist attack; people stepped into aeroplanes with trepidation and preferred not to if it could be avoided. There clearly existed an enemy capable of large-scale impact, and an enemy which had established equivalence, but the enemy hadn't revealed itself. The question that had to be answered was: given what is understood of the procedures and ethics of warfare how could this war (that had been announced and commenced already) be engaged with?

The answer was obvious: since the enemy wasn't going to declare themselves and thereby become obvious, the enemy had to be retrospectively constructed. In some sense the enemy had to be *interpreted* from the events of 11 September in such a way that it could at least be *perceived* that an enemy had been identified and the war engaged with by the United States. A war announced and begun by a terrorist act had to be responded to with force, as behoves warring parties. Military action (preferably with the appearance of being of a conventional mould) is the most emphatic kind of force at the disposal of any political state. But given the uncertainties regarding the enemy any military action against any plausible target would ethically be a complicated matter. But the *show* of military force and a *perception* of war on conventional grounds was deemed necessary as a response, not least because such a conventional war would itself be a morally effective counter to indirect terrorist warfare, with all the repugnance at the loss of innocent lives that the latter instinctively entails. Conventional warfare has *strong associations* with notions of legitimacy whereas terrorist warfare by its nature subverts existing notions of legitimacy. Such a conventional-warfare-like response would also be reassuring to the people of the United States and other countries that might feel threatened by terrorist warfare – something understandable would be *perceived* as being done. At the very least, conventional warfare is reassuring because of its ritualistic nature. A conventional-warfare-like response could therefore be regarded as both a way of accepting the claim to equivalence that the terrorist attack had announced, and of expressing a disdain for that claim. And yet, despite the fact that a *show* and consequent *perception* of a conventional-warfare-like response would itself give some moral validity to that response, there still remained the tricky moral matter of finding a target. In this case no target could be unambiguously held to be accountable for what had happened; the attacks of 11 September had been engineered in such a manner that even if there *seemed* to exist a great deal of plausibility about the identity of the perpetrators, no amount of proof or trust could be called upon to get everyone to be *convinced* that this has been *conclusively established* (especially across national boundaries). It was patently obvious (as the italicised words in this paragraph show) that the response to this declaration and commencement of war on

11 September would be a complex play on perspectives, a complicated negotiation of appearances.

The two kinds of war that emerged were a result of this. The best way to deal with the paradoxes presented by the 11 September attacks for the responding party was to separate the ethical and the procedural spheres of the war. The moral complexities attached to the procedure of responsive military action could be directed towards the 'war against international terrorism' in abstract; the procedural complexities of the 'war against international terrorism' in abstract could be directed towards the responsive military action. Any questioning of the one could be answered by reference to the other despite the fact that the two areas – the two kinds of war – were actually quite distinct; and the result would be that distinctions would gradually get blurred, a certain confusion would inevitably follow, the two wars would merge into each other and become one war which one might feel uncomfortable about but which could be conducted effectively. The two wars that effectively allowed for different spheres of dealing with ethical and procedural issues (not too neatly differentiated, more in the interest of blurring boundaries between contradictory procedural and ethical demands) simply created space for the play of perspectives, the negotiation of appearances, to be handled smoothly.

The strategies behind the attacks of 11 September and the two-pronged response ('war against international terrorism' in abstract and military action against specific groups and the nations that harbour them) are reasonably clear. But the blurring of distinctions and the ensuing confusion that these were devised for cannot and should not be swallowed wholesale. There were two wars – and two kinds of warfare – involved here, and naturally both had their distinct ethical and procedural nuances. At least conceptually, these need to be resolved separately before being allowed to feed into each other. That is what the rest of this study is devoted to.

On 8 October United States and British forces started bombing Afghanistan. Along with the bombs packets of food were also dropped for the dislocated and starving common people of Afghanistan. Humanitarian aid organisations were predicting a humanitarian catastrophe of significant proportions in Afghanistan.

4 'War Against International Terrorism' in Abstractions

About five days into the bombing of Afghanistan fears that the 'propaganda war' was possibly as important as the military action beset the United States and Britain. British Prime Minister Tony Blair was by now recognised as the special envoy of the United States to keep the coalition against terrorism going – especially within the Middle East. He upped the stakes on propaganda and flew around the Middle East busily reassuring reluctant and tentative allies, getting qualified support in some places and being brushed aside in others (in Saudi Arabia, for instance) – but primarily being *seen* as friendly and at home with all. He even expressed his misgiving about the propaganda situation quite openly. It had to be done: bin Laden had released a few videos that were broadcast around the world with some effect. He was seen sitting apparently coolly in the midst of an arid landscape, exhorting Muslims around the world to rise against the United States, promising more terror (which might be read as accepting responsibility for the terrorist attacks of 11 September, but then again it might not), in a calm monotone. United States intelligence wondered whether there might not be secret codes in these videos, passing on instructions to the 'international terrorist' network. By 12 October the United States government had persuaded the media not to broadcast these video messages. By 13 October similar warnings were being passed on to the British media. Taliban officials were seen on the media talking about civilian casualties due to the bombing with the faintest touch of regret. Riots had broken out in Palestine and Pakistan and Indonesia and Nigeria and had to be tackled by some savage policing. More food packages were dropped over Afghanistan and a lot more bombs. The United States issued veiled threats to other alleged harbourers of terrorists (Malaysia was surprised to find itself amongst those covered by such threats), and postured more openly against another enemy of longer standing – Saddam Hussein in Iraq. But the 'propaganda war' couldn't be fought by threats alone, or by the intrepid Blair alone. By 12 October it was also announced that the United States was going to force a resolution of the Palestinian problem – the main source of grievance in the Middle East it appeared – by putting pressure on their long-standing ally Israel to concede a dual government in Jerusalem. The hardline Ariel Sharon was bitter. It wasn't at all clear that Israel would concede anything of the sort. But it was deemed a good move in the propaganda war. Tony Blair said he would see to it that Afghanistan was not abandoned after the war. General Pervez Musharraf gave out that he was worried that the Taliban would be replaced within Afghanistan by the Northern Alliance, who were already fighting a long and till then apparently futile war against the Taliban. Pakistan had some legitimate doubts about the credibility of the Northern Alliance. But the aftermath of the 'war against international terrorism' seemed still distant: all those bombs didn't appear to do much to loosen bin Laden's or al-Quaeda's or the Taliban's hold in Afghanistan, and nor did those food packets do much to help the trapped and terrified civilians and refugees there.

Two interrelated wars – one with arms and the other with abstractions – carried on through October 2001, starkly distinct at times and merging into each other at others. The curious combination of lots of bombs and some food packages continued to drop on Afghanistan. By the end of October 3,000 bombs had been dropped, some of them cluster bombs which do not target anything particularly precisely. The contents of the food packets turned out to be more cosmetic than substantial, and the packets were labelled as gifts from the United States in English, Spanish and French. The food packets, it was reported, were about the same size and colour as the cluster bombs and could easily be confused.

Meanwhile the possibility had faded altogether of any peace between Israel and Palestine being engineered by the United States, with hostilities reaching a new low, and Ariel Sharon in a defiant mood at what he saw as the United States's appeasement policy towards Arab states supporting the Palestinians.

After 11 September any 'war against international terrorism' in abstract was a war that to a large extent had to be fought *at* the level of abstractions. The need to fight it appeared because retaliatory military action, a conventional use of force, could engage with any specific target only through a haze of scepticism and recriminations (however certain of their target the United States professed herself to be). It was therefore largely a war with and between perspectives and theories and rhetoric, but all these were such in this context that at every moment they threatened to concretise into frighteningly material acts and counter-acts, to merge into and emerge out of violence in the happening world. Such a war pertained to the political world, as perspectives and theories and rhetoric always pertain to a stable or relatively stable political world but only more *intensely*: a war at the level of abstractions makes abstractions weapons of more than usual potency, wields these weapons to overcome the initial equivalence that is perceived and recognised in the enemy, exerts abstractions with force that can subdue and overcome. There enters violence in the brandishing of abstractions that could, at any moment, break into material violence or make violence the bridge between theory and practice. There is an *intensification* characteristic of war roughly along the lines described by Wright.[1]

Two questions need to be considered before I give any elucidation of what such a 'war against international terrorism' might entail: What are the connotations of 'international terrorism' especially when spoken of after 11 September? and What are the advantages and disadvantages from the perspective of each warring party respectively in having these connotations attached?

Connotations of 'international terrorism' especially after 11 September: by that I do not allude to the obvious meaning of the phrase (I have to some extent discussed the vagaries and possibilities of that already – political violence across national boundaries with unconventional war strategies, etc.) but to the unexpected and non-obvious senses that have deliberately or inadvertently been absorbed into that phrase. That such an absorption of non-obvious senses occurs is of course largely because of the nature of the attacks of 11 September, because of the fact that their causes and motivations were not announced but had to be interpreted in retrospect, and interpreted with a view to bringing the broadest and most persuasive positioning of the abstract enemy into collision with the narrowest and inevitably questionable positioning of the specific enemy target that could be militarily acted against. The following are the points that come to mind in this connection:

a. 'International terrorism' need not be strictly understood as political violence that is perpetrated from one location and directed at another that rests within a different national boundary. In some sense *any* act of terrorism can now be thought of as an act of 'international terrorism'. Several practical arguments can be adduced to support this view. Even acts of terrorism which are conducted internally and are directed against a particular political state may now resort to using means that are a matter of international concern, for example, kidnapping tourists to bring outside pressure to bear upon the state in question.[2] More importantly just as there has come to evolve an increasingly coherent global network of informational, economic and political coordination, it is suspected that there must correspondingly (necessarily correspondingly) have developed a more coherent globalisation of terrorism. Even localised acts of terrorism pertinent to local conditions may be linked to arms deals, economic transactions, information exchange and pragmatic collaboration with other terrorist groups across national boundaries, or at a global level.

b. That *any* act of terrorism may now be regarded as 'international terrorism' also rests on certain conceptual propositions. In the course of the Cold War most 'international terrorist' attacks were conducted – and even if they weren't, were interpreted as being conducted – at the behest of the superpowers and their allies. This understanding and interpretation involved an attribution of ideological motivations that rested on broad abstractions and loose jargonising which could not ultimately be located strictly within specific national boundaries. Ideological positions are usually argued with some notion of appealing to or defending universal human values and interests. However, as I have mentioned above, such interpretations of 'international terrorist' attacks were generally based on clear claims and easy attributions, and, along with the Cold War situation, this gave the overall picture a certain clarity. There has thus come to prevail a culture of ideological attributions to terrorist acts that necessarily transcends national boundaries and affect general human interests and well-being. However, the lack of clarity regarding the picture out of which attacks such as those of 11 September emerge means that the methods of such attributions have taken on a markedly different quality. On the one hand, the effort to fix these events into the mould of existing understanding (in terms of ideological attributions) is evidenced. On the other hand though, a stronger-than-usual focus has to be laid not so much on oppositional ideology as a *source* but on the *means* deployed in its name (terror as a political weapon in itself). These are issues I deal with at some length below.

c. Also within the sphere of conceptual understanding, both the scale of casualties and the context of the attacks (as I have observed in Chapter 1) have now made a considerable difference to the connotations of 'international terrorism'. I do not intend to repeat myself on this – but a few ancillary points to the ones that I have made before are worth fleshing out. That 'international terrorism' can declare and initiate war in such a devastating fashion on a superpower like the United States has very significant effects on the world economy. The concentration of trading and trading resources in the United States, the fact that almost any significant multinational corporation has to have very active operations within that country, the manner in which the US dollar has come to be regarded as a sort of stable world currency and the degree to which it provides the peg against which other currencies are assessed, the degree to which the government collaborates and complements these autonomous economic institutions, and (most essentially) the underlying perception of security that had enabled these to flourish in the United States have been disturbed to the extent that 'international terrorism' is now bound to be regarded as a more pervasive and material *economic* factor. The closing and reopening of the New York stock exchange after 11 September marked that period of transition in which the new status of 'international terrorism' as such became fully factored into the working of the world economy. The effects of the terrorist attacks on certain sectors of the world economy were immediately evident – the losses to certain concerns (e.g. insurance companies, air travel and tourist industries) and gains to some (e.g. telecommunications and broadcasting concerns, defence and security industries); the measures taken by the United States and other Western governments to monitor fiscal movements with a view to curbing resources available to terrorists; the redrawing of political alignments and therefore of aid (thus Pakistani President Musharraf's agreement to join the 'coalition against terrorism' was rewarded by the lifting of sanctions and by generous financial benefits); and so on. The long-term effects are yet to be fully gauged but will undoubtedly be significant. Does this mean that political monitoring of international fiscal movements will now become more thorough than it was in the past? How would the attacks impact on the global economic slowdown and recession that economists and industrialists had been discussing for a while before 11 September? How long-term will the effects on the affected sectors be? (Are defence budgets going to rise? Is air travel going to change significantly?) How will the attacks and the consequent 'war against international terrorism' influence international moves towards market liberalisation and economic cooperation? – and so on. At any rate it is clear that 'international terrorism' is now a significant economic factor and that those thought of as 'international terrorists' can also be regarded as significant economic actors.

d. Despite the increased sense of pervasiveness and significance that 'international terrorism' has acquired after 11 September, it has managed to retain, indeed even enhance, its air of being a threat from without. The boundaries from which the *outside* and the *inside* are determined are of course not coincidental with any legalistic understanding of national boundaries – these stretch or shrink or blur according to the already hazy abstractions in the context within which they are raised. The West has regrouped against its rejuvenated significant *other*, no longer the East and Soviet-led communism but the Arab world. But what is the Arab world? Not quite the Orient of before, but a spasm from within that semi-fantasised and semiconstructed space. Not quite a collection of nations, for national interests and alignments as understood in the West are not quite what are seen to bind that Arab world together – if bound together they are. Let us be blunt about it: in the West the Arab world is a faith (Islam) and a race (Arabs) as well as a tract within a continent (the Middle East). Never mind that none of these actually matches on to the others: there are people of many races who adhere to that faith, and people of many faiths who inhabit that territory, and the faith itself is far from being a homogeneous and evenly constituted and internally harmonious formation. But that Arab world, so understood (faith, race, territory) spills out of itself into the heart of the West itself. People of 'Arabic appearance' walk on the streets of every major metropolis in the United States and Europe: the Arab world is a racial presence within the West and racists feel called upon to rise to the occasion. People of the Islamic faith practise their rituals and wear their characteristic garments (beards or veils as the case may be), as do people of so many other faiths, throughout the world and naturally including the Western countries: the Arab world is a religious-cultural presence and xenophobes too rise to the occasion. The rising of the racists and xenophobes itself blurs rather than clarifies the racial and religious-cultural boundaries: for how many born and bred white or black Americans and Europeans can tell apart Indians and Pakistanis and Afghans and Iraqis, or Chinese and Thai and Burmese and Indonesians? Or, for that matter, identify and distinguish between an Indonesian Muslim and an Indonesian Christian or Hindu; a Nigerian Muslim and a Bosnian Muslim and a Malaysian Muslim and an Afghan Muslim; and so on. Racists and xenophobes turn the *inside* with inevitable fascist instinct into a homogenous racial and/or religious-cultural national formation. Those who are concerned with liberal democratic government of course know better: suitable antiracist legislation is called into effect, racial and xenophobic attacks are denounced, political bridges are deliberately and theatrically built with Muslim communities *within* and where possible *without*. And yet some form of state support for the rejuvenated xenophobia and racism is unavoidable because the Arab world is constructed as it is, the Arab world is that combination of faith, race and territory from the liberal democratic West's reductive point of view. So, in the name of justified security-consciousness it becomes possible for air stewards and passengers to ask people of 'Arab appearance' to leave without facing a racial discrimination suit; it becomes quite all right to be suspicious of what an obviously Muslim person is doing anywhere; it becomes okay to manipulate asylum laws so that foreigners (*outside*) carry identity cards so as to be always identifiable as foreigners; and civil liberties can be played with to make those *outside* and yet uncomfortably *within* (often European and American citizens, generally long-established and productive members of society, usually breaking no law of the land) more gratingly *visible* than usual; and to speak of Muslims as *them* as opposed to *us*. 'International terrorism' is always from *outside* but the *outside* need not be too far away. The *inside* gets narrower to keep 'international terrorism' *outside*, or to keep 'international terrorism' *international*.

These somewhat renewed connotations of 'international terrorism' have certain advantages and disadvantages for each of the warring parties respectively. From the perspective of the United States and the Western and other collaborators in the 'war against international terrorism' the following points are noteworthy:

a. The immediate indistinctness of the precise source of the terrorist
    attacks of 11 September, of the actual perpetrators, could be
    countered by interpreting them as being a symptom of a wider
    'international terrorism', which is materially pervasive and
    globalised. This enabled a focus on the *means* by which the
    attacks announced and commenced war (political terror) as being
    the target, rather than the *agents* (the specific perpetrators) as
    being the targets. That in turn led to two immediate advantages:
    one, that whoever could be *suspected* of the attacks could be made
    a legitimate target, for even if responsibility for these particular
    attacks could not be firmly established and proved, at least their
    association with such means in general would still be considered
    to be heinous enough to deserve punishment; and two, that
    given the kind of global linkages and cooperation that are alleged
    of 'international terrorism', along with the focus on the means of
    political terror, a large number of ideologically and economically
    and ethically unpalatable alignments and organisations (from a
    capitalist Western liberal democratic perspective) could also be
    targeted with less opposition than usual. At the level of abstrac-
    tion at which the connotations of 'international terrorism'
    enumerated above came into play, interrogations of these
    objectives were unlikely to occur. Things were too abstractly and
    theoretically mixed up. The only position which showed some
    evidence of trying to unravel the claims of legitimacy which
    attended announcements of such objectives was that which
    approached this matter from a legal angle, as a matter of jurispru-
    dence. On the whole, voices that attempted to take this approach
    were largely muted and disregarded. Where somewhat careworn
    or defiant Muslim clerics and community leaders within the West
    asked that more of a legal process be followed or complained that
    there was too little of this in the response to the attacks of 11
    September, it was easily assumed that this was simply the
    defensive squeak of followers of an ideology or faith that had
    revealed the worst of itself. When the rare international law
    scholar published a brief letter or feature querying the legal
    position of the 'war against international terrorism' it was
    regarded as rather precious legalistic hairsplitting. The only legal
    consideration that made any impression on proceedings was that
    which concerned where and how bin Laden and his associates
    should be judged if captured. In effect the post-11-September
    characterisation of 'international terrorism' has been put beyond

the pale of normal law. This again is not inconsistent with the legal abnormality of war situations, but it is worth noting clearly. *'International terrorism' became in this war situation a target which transcends legal procedure, and remains so.* This is particularly worth noting since it showed a decisive and unashamed departure on the part of the West, and especially of the United States, from what was received wisdom (even if seldom followed in practice) about policy regarding terrorism before 11 September. In a revealing book by Stansfield Turner, former chief of central intelligence in the United States, on United States strategy apropos terrorism, it is observed that though the United States has routinely made deals with terrorists, and has often resorted to assassinations, punitive military attacks, covert operations, and so on against terrorists, 'legal recourse is the option most compatible with American values'.[3] That 'international terrorism' had gradually begun to be regarded by the United States as that peculiar sphere of activity that could be acted against without legal process was evident since the retaliatory bombing of Libya in 1986, but military strikes still continued to be presented as a regretful last resort where judicial process is difficult. Very shortly before the 11 September attacks an interesting article by Michele L. Malvesti was already starting to formalise an 'explanatory theory of the conditions under which the United States decides to move beyond the standard judicial approach and initiative to a use of force via overt military action to an incident of anti-US international terrorism'.[4] Now, in one precipitate move, such reflections of what justifies action beyond judicial remedy have become irrelevant – judicial process is not an issue here. Those suspected of being associated with 'international terrorism' are, even in being suspected, put beyond judicial process and judged guilty.

b. Targeting 'international terrorism' in abstract allows for the targeting of *any* act of political violence which can somehow be interpreted as being from *outside*; targeting this abstraction allows for an indiscriminate focus on means (political terror) at the expense of discrimination regarding perpetrators and their reasons. Now the *outside* is primarily the Arab world, and somehow all manifestations of 'international terrorism' can be percolated into a concentrated brew – all manifestations of 'international terrorism' can be condensed into the monstrous partnership of tyranny (habourers of terrorists) and the fanatic ('international terrorists') emanating out of the Arab world. To make these potent abstractions all the more efficacious, that heady brew is distilled further to yield a vial of foul condensate: a condensate of evil genii, the icons of 'international terrorism'. It all boils down to monstrous individuals – or at any rate to the images of monstrous individuals. After 11 September there must have been a person called Osama bin Laden hidden among the mountains in Afghanistan who was suspected of having masterminded the most momentous act of mass murder in recent memory. But one sometimes began to doubt the reality of this, for bin Laden had also turned into a myth – and nowhere more so than in the psyche of the West. Bin Laden was there only by inference: his speech seen in a video recording was more than a speech, it was also a petrifying echo which spoke to all the terrorists of the world and perhaps all the fanatics of the world, and had to be censored; he was like a ghost in the ravines, and the great might of the West was unsure that he could be flushed out; his signature was more than a signature, it was a bugle call and a clue to the mind of the enemy as a whole; a whole alternative world economy seemed to revolve around him, and untold wealth had passed on to him and his associates without anyone having noticed it before; people who spoke in his name were somehow no more than automata, the robotic messengers of cybermaster bin Laden; the need to neutralise bin Laden was enough to justify the displacement and terrorising of millions of Afghans, and the incidental killing of a large number of Afghan civilians; eliminating bin Laden would not only *avenge* the terrorist attacks of 11 September, it would also erase 'international terrorism' itself to a large measure. But only to a large measure – because there are still a few other monsters out there – Saddam Hussein, and those 22 terrorists on the FBI's most-wanted list – and the many unnamed countries which harbour them. Opposed to this condensation of 'international terrorism' emanating from the blur of the Arab world is another foul condensation. This is the antidote emanating from an equally blurred West, from the psyche that defines its *inside* as opposed to that *outside*, where the tyrannies and fanatics of the Arab world have their ostensible existence. This is the realm of freedom and democracy, beset by tyrannical and fanatical monsters from the Arab world. The condensation of 'international terrorism' after 11 September, that has been conducted largely within the psyche of the West, has enabled and is complemented by a virtuous intensification of social integration within the West. Extending liberal understanding and pity and assistance to the poor victims of tyranny in the Arab world is as much part of this virtuousness as is the resolution to defend aggressively the freedom and democracy that is the possession of the West and the largesse of the West. This condensation of the antidote leaves some unpleasant dregs within a residual amnesia. Within that residual amnesia lies the nascent but omnipresent neofascism of the West; the evidence of a systemic neoimperialism whereby the West retains her self-interests against all *outsides*; and so on. But these are not worth mentioning here – they lack equivalence with 'international terrorism', they are irrelevant to the concern with 'international terrorism', these are the concerns of self-righteous and ultimately spurious socialists and greens who prefer not to live in the 'real world'. What the tyranny and fanaticism behind 'international terrorism' does have equivalence with (and this is a relationship of pure opposition) is freedom and democracy, and that, irrespective of all minor blemishes, *is* the possession and largesse of the West. The great advantage of the 'war against international terrorism' in abstract is that this is a war that can be fought within the mind of the West in terms of its perceived *self* or *inside* (which claims freedom and democracy) against the perceived *other* on the *outside* (to which is attributed tyranny and fanaticism). But this West of the mind is more than the West on any atlas (it is a set of universal values and desires), just as the Arab world of the mind is more than any Arab world on an atlas (it is also a set of universal fears and revulsions). The war of abstractions at this level is a complex negotiation of material strategies and ephemera, and I return to it later in focusing on the usage of the terms *fanaticism* and *democracy*.

c. 'International terrorism' is pervasive and yet *outside* – in the Arab world; but that *outside* is also sometimes *inside* – inside the Western domain, though still outside racial and cultural boundaries. 'International terrorism' is an economic factor which affects international and therefore national industries and budgets in a way that cannot be avoided. 'International terrorism' has to be tackled outside legal process, the ordinary recourse and security of legal protection must be considered in some sense unequal to what is needed. 'International terrorism' renders it necessary that while the state continues to come down heavily upon xenophobic and racist acts on the streets it also gives some institutional sanction to what must be perceived as xenophobic and racist policy. These effects of 'international terrorism' in abstract after 11 September were bound to rebound into the domestic sphere within the West – in the United States, where the attacks took place and where the weight of these effects was felt most heavily, this kept the intensity of terror constant while the 'war against international terrorism' went through its predictable process. There were all sorts of paradoxes involved in this. It was the psychology of terror that in the first place obligated the state to reassert its strength by responding aggressively to the declaration and commencement of war on 11 September. Even a minimal conception of a political state (which the American polity has often expressed admiration for), such as Hayek's or Nozick's,[5] enjoins on the state a (suitably institutionally compliant) protective and policing role. That is the least a political state is morally expected to perform: there is no question that if a psychology of terror is created by a formation other than the state itself, the state will have to reassert its credentials by combating it aggressively. But how can it do so without also perpetuating the psychology of terror, without in a manner of speaking taking over the manipulation of that psychology itself? The political state in the United States fell in with this manipulation with double effect: it protected the *inside* by directing its 'war against international terrorism' *outside*, and it conducted its 'war against international terrorism' *outside* on all fronts by holding up the psychology of terror that prevailed *inside* as justification – thereby manipulating that psychology itself. Fear *inside* makes it expedient that the state asserts itself; fear *inside* consolidates the position of the state as state; fear *inside* leads to a desire for a stronger state; and the state that wants to appear equal to the situation and as strong as necessary and prove itself needs fear *inside*. Each act of punitive aggression against 'international terrorism' in the past has resulted in support for the state's role as protector and aggressor against an *outside*:

> Polls in the wake of the strikes showed 77 per cent of US citizens supported the raid on Libya and 66 per cent supported the strikes against Iraq. One poll following the two-pronged strike in Sudan and Afghanistan indicated 66 per cent supported the operation while a second showed support at 80

per cent. Accordingly, US public opinion has strongly favoured the US 'power' approach to countering terrorism.[6]

After 11 September it seemed that public opinion was even more compliant than usual. At first it was reported that 78 per cent of Americans were in support of military action against Afghanistan. A week into the bombing, and with a strong sense of its futility becoming rapidly evident, a figure in excess of 90 per cent was quoted by some sources. Allowing for the vagaries of opinion polls, the domestic consent to military strikes apparently at least held steady over an extended period, even if it did not actually increase. The recently formed Republican government of George Bush continued to enjoy previously unimaginable support and collaboration from all sectors of the population of the United States. The nation continued to show every evidence of holding its breath for another 'international terrorist' attack and was constantly warned that such attacks were on their way. Even two months after the terrorist attacks of 11 September the United States had not achieved any diminution of terror on the *inside*, and wasn't particularly trying to allay the fears of her citizens.

So, the connotations that 'international terrorism' acquired, or acquired more strongly, after 11 September (listed earlier in this chapter) had certain advantages and disadvantages for the United States and the alignment of her collaborators and supporters in the 'war against international terrorism' in abstract. Such advantages and disadvantages were obviously not manifested on one side alone – advantages and disadvantages from this understanding of 'international terrorism' in abstract devolved on the other side too. The other side however is not an easy one to characterise. In the interests of theoretical rigour I characterise the other side at four levels: the immediately unknown perpetrators of the 11 September attacks; the immediate and most likely suspects, bin Laden and the al-Quaeda network (on this distinction between perpetrators and bin Laden/al-Quaeda, especially in the context of developments in December 2001, I have more to say in Chapter 6); the Taliban government in Afghanistan; and other groups or networks of terrorists (whatever causes they stood for) who might get drawn into the 'war against international terrorism'. I characterise these four levels separately, not to cast doubt on the largely accepted coincidence of the first two, but because it is precisely fissures along these lines that translated into the advantages and disadvantages in question in the 'war against international terrorism' that followed 11 September. The points pertinent to the latter follow (in a more speculative and theoretical fashion than the above since I haven't the advantage of being able to gauge movements and reactions within the Middle East at the time of writing):

a. The breadth of 'international terrorism' as understood after 11 September shrouded the perpetrator *as* perpetrator. The perpetrators could enter the forum of the war of abstractions *as* perpetrators only if it could be proved that they were so. Proving in this instance was not a matter of finding incontrovertible evidence which could stand up in a court of law, it was more importantly a matter of being able to create an environment where all parties who were in a position to observe proceedings could feel convinced that those who were accused were also guilty. Thus, the fact that acts of 'international terrorism' were now considered beyond legal recourse did not necessarily mean that the perpetrators could not be held accountable as such (or that this could not be proved); the perpetrators could still have been held accountable if such an environment was created that disbelief was suspended among all parties. That proving the guilt of bin Laden and al-Quaeda in a strictly legal sense might be difficult was suspected from the beginning – there was no neutral investigating party who could be believed if it presented such proof. It would have been impossible for the United States to *prove* legalistically that bin Laden and the al-Quaeda network were responsible for the terrorist attacks of 11 September (unless they accepted responsibility and presented the proof themselves), simply because it was the United States who would have to act as the investigating party, and any evidence they produced would be suspect pretty much before it was produced. Thus, when it was initially reported that a car with some sort of al-Quaeda manual was found outside the airport from which one of the ill-fated aeroplanes was hijacked for the 11 September attacks, it seemed suspiciously convenient. Facts about the movements of the suicidal terrorists immediately responsible for the attacks were traced and appeared in the papers for a while, but few felt convinced that any direct and believable link to bin Laden and al-Quaeda had been established. These legalistic efforts were probably doomed already: the United States and the West had presumed bin Laden's and al-Quaeda's guilt so quickly and with such single-mindedness that any proof of guilt presented after that was bound to appear to be unbelievably convenient, and probably spurious. In effect, the difficulties of overcoming scepticism about the guilt of the accused party was a tough matter. However, it is possible that if the United States and her allies had persisted in such efforts to find what appeared to be legally valid proof, at some point an environment might well have been created whereby the relevant observers would simply have been inclined to suspend their scepticism. It is evident now that somewhere in the move from those early investigative efforts to the commencement of the 'war against international terrorism' in terms of military action, the impetus to prove anything had diminished. With the above-discussed connotations of 'international terrorism' in mind, from the United States's and the West's point of view the need to unmask the perpetrator *as* perpetrator had receded into the background, and with it the possibility of creating an environment whereby scepticism could have been suspended even if proof positive couldn't be immediately produced. The attitude of the United States towards bin Laden and al-Quaeda was: 'We are convinced that you are the perpetrator of the 11 September attacks and do not need to wait for any proof before punishing you, and even if there unexpectedly emerges reason to believe that you are not, you are still a representative of "international terrorism" and undoubtedly responsible for other serious attacks and will have deserved your punishment; we regard your punishment as just retribution and an example to all terrorists everywhere, and even if it is not strictly just retribution for the 11 September attacks it is still an example.' Meanwhile there was little further discussion about that alleged car and manual outside the airport, or about the movements and backgrounds of the suicidal killers, nor was there any other circumstantial evidence. That was all very well, but it didn't make for an environment where all relevant observers could feel wholly inclined to suspend their scepticism. It is unarguable that the perpetrators of the 11 September attacks *as* perpetrators – the people who were directly and unquestionably responsible – had effectively disappeared from the precincts of 'the war against international terrorism', shrouded under the cover of the blanket term 'international terrorism', which was actually targeted. There remained, of course, the possibility that suitable evidence of bin Laden's and al-Quaeda's guilt would eventually emerge and that the whole 'war against international terrorism' would be considered just and necessary in retrospect – but that seemed an unlikely possibility when the 'war against international terrorism' got under way, and it would not in any case invalidate, as far as one could see, any of the above-described connotations that 'international terrorism' had already acquired.

b. Bin Laden and his lieutenants used the above-listed connotations of 'international terrorism', together with the fact that the perpetrators *as* perpetrators had effectively disappeared, to expand their sense of effectiveness as far as possible. They found, and I suspect had anticipated that they would find, that the haziness and inclusiveness of the targets and the lingering scepticisms that wouldn't go away in the 'war against international terrorism' allowed them to expand their sphere of effectiveness by claiming a series of associations. To begin with, bin Laden and his supporters associated themselves with the equivalence that was contained in the announcement and commencement of the war through the 11 September attacks. By neither denying nor claiming responsibility for the attacks, they allowed the perception that they were the masterminds of those attacks, or were certainly perfectly capable of the sort of attacks whereby equivalence could be maintained with a state as powerful as the United States. And yet by neither denying nor claiming responsibility they also left the perpetrator-*as*-perpetrator issue open, with the resut that the onus of moral responsibility for what the United States did to them remained firmly on the latter's shoulders. Hints were given by bin Laden and his lieutenants that further terrorist acts in a similar mould would be directed against the United States if it kept up its aggression in the Arab world, but always ambiguously worded so that they could be read either as threats that al-Quaeda would carry out in response to this specific military action, or as spontaneous general expressions of Islamic and Arab disgruntlement at the iniquities of United States foreign policy. That bin Laden and company associated themselves with Islam per se was of course not in the least surprising, but there was no doubt that the construction of the 11 September attacks as 'international terrorist' attacks emanating indiscriminately from the Arab world outside had assisted in the effectiveness of this association. Bin Laden was clearly fully cognisant of the Western notion of the Arab world as a racial/cultural/territorial construction – and that those in the West had scared themselves by finding the Arab world *inside* as much as *outside* – and, whenever possible, exploited those fears fully. Statements from bin Laden spokesmen exhorting Muslims to rise *everywhere*, not least within the West, and warning Muslims in the West to stay away from high-rise buildings and avoid aeroplanes, may not have succeeded in rousing anything much in the Muslim communities within the West except fear for their immediate security – but they were weapons that could work best because xenophobes and racists could use them, and more importantly because the state could be relied on to give some necessary sanction to institutional xenophobia and racism. Bin Laden also succeeded in associating his claim of fighting for Islam with specific and long-drawn-out conflicts in which he had shown little interest before, thereby aligning himself with interest groups which did not coincide with whatever form of extremist Islamic ideology he espoused (which remains unclear). This was possible to a large extent because it could be accommodated within the target 'international terrorism'. Chief amongst these was his championing of the Palestinian cause (though aggressively fought in recent years by the Islamic Hamas, it has never been an exclusively Islamic cause) against the Israelis (who had themselves initially welcomed the 'war against international terrorism' in the hope that Hamas terrorists could be included in that category, only to find the tables turned on themselves). This last move in making associations appeared for a while to have worked particularly well for bin Laden in the war of abstractions. If the conservative Ariel Sharon could have been persuaded to reopen negotiations with the obdurate Yasser Arafat under pressure from the United States, that could well have been a diplomatic coup that bin Laden could claim as his. It is clear, I think, that irrespective of the outcome of the military action, bin Laden's bid to play with associations arising from 'international terrorism' succeeded well enough to ensure that his mythic stature – as hero or monster – would hold the imagination of all parties for years to come.

c. For the Taliban there were more disadvantages than advantages in finding themselves squarely within the remit of the targeting of 'international terrorism'. The Taliban might have initially felt that this was an unexpected opportunity to gain a different profile: from being the most repressive and authoritarian and isolated regime of our time – looked on as a kind of bizarre and dangerous experiment even by neighbouring states with Islamic theocratic constitutions – to becoming victimised representatives of Islam. The Taliban had tried to assume the mantle of Islam as far as possible – but the associations that bin Laden and al-Quaeda were able to make more or less effortlessly and to such effect did not attach to the Taliban in the same way. There was an enormous difference between bin Laden and al-Quaeda claiming the mantle of Islam and the Taliban claiming it: the former was a terrorist organisation which had a definite anti-establishment air about it which could appeal to the unthinking bigot and could seep out with mythic power within the fears and longings of a populace at large, but the Taliban represented, however indifferently and indeed tyrannously, a sovereign state which first had to deal with and be dealt with by other sovereign states – many of whom could claim theocratic legitimacy *and* international sanction as the Taliban could not. So rioters who had taken to the streets in the name of Islam in Palestine, Nigeria, Pakistan, Indonesia and elsewhere had done so by expressing support for the myth of bin Laden, for the reality of the suffering people of Afghanistan, but very seldom indeed for the Taliban regime as such. Meanwhile the Taliban faced the disapproval of other far better established Islamic states which were unwilling to fall out with the United States and were not convinced that Taliban was an important enough international player to justify such a falling out: arraigned against the Taliban's particular claim to Islamic legitimacy were the more ponderous and long established theocratic credentials of Saudi Arabia and Iran and even the formerly well-disposed Pakistan. The Taliban tried to capitalise on evidence (that emerged by mid-October) of considerable numbers of civilian casualties due to misdirected American missiles. The consequent claim made by the Taliban (as representing a sovereign state) that it was the victim of United States repression, however, did not work well. Such had been the human rights abuses and oppression of the Taliban regime that any relationship that might have been perceived between it as state and the Afghan people has been eroded: it was fairly clear that the Taliban had never been good for the people of Afghanistan. Military action leading to a humanitarian disaster in Afghanistan might, as the United States admitted, be 'regrettable' – but outside pockets of bitter anti-American sentiment or the blindest adherence to extremist

Islam this hadn't brought any credit to the Taliban. That it had not brought any credit to the Taliban effectively meant that, despite Pakistan's initial reservations, the whole situation worked in favour of the Northern Alliance.

d. To determine how other terrorist groups and networks have gained or lost in this 'war against international terrorism' more time is needed. Some inkling of this – in a necessarily speculative and tentative fashion – may emerge in pondering on the anthrax attacks which were reported in a concentrated fashion roughly between 10 and 18 October. Two cases of the rare viral infection, anthrax, were initially reported in Florida. This was considered to be suspicious, and since the 'war against international terrorism' was in the air there were naturally some suspicions that these cases might have been deliberately caused by terrorist use of biological weapons. It was mentioned in several reports that Iraq had long been suspected of building up a biological weapons arsenal (such allegations have been used routinely to justify the economic sanctions that have been in place against Iraq, as well as several bombing raids over that unfortunate country, since the Gulf War). However no evidence was reported linking these first two cases explicitly to terrorist activity emanating from the Arab world. Meanwhile United States intelligence warned the American people to be prepared for further serious terrorist attacks (possibly using biological weapons) while the 'war against international terrorism' was under way. About a week after these first cases were reported in the media, a spate of letters containing a white scented powder were received within the United States and a large number of other countries across the world. The targets were not especially carefully chosen (some media personnel and a senator in the United States were unsurprisingly highlighted in the media). Most of these letters originated within the United States, but not all. In a few cases these letters were proved to contain anthrax spores, but the greater number of such letters turned out to be hoaxes. There was widespread disruption in postal services, people (especially in the United States) felt ever more vulnerable, and more intensive security measures were instituted in all the threatened countries. It was also reported that such anthrax spores were actually quite difficult to produce, and that the United States intelligence suspected that the resources of some foreign government ('international terrorism' always comes from *outside*) might have gone into these anthrax attacks.

The al-Quaeda network obviously came to mind – but whatever foreign governments might have been involved, certainly the Taliban could not be implicated. Iraq seemed to many in the West to be a possible source: a question to that effect put by reporters to the Iraqi foreign minister was answered with a succinct 'bullshit'. The question was mooted of other possible terrorist-hosting biological-weapon-stocking anti-American governments: Egypt? Libya? North Korea? But by this time it was apparent that such accusations were no more than wild and quite possibly irresponsible speculations. Meanwhile bombings continued unabated in Afghanistan and the United States and Britain were contemplating sending in ground troops. The media cooled down about the anthrax attacks, only to be reminded by 22 October that this was far from over with the death from anthrax of two postal workers in Washington. Something important had already been demonstrated by this time. The undiscriminating sense of pervasiveness of 'international terrorism' meant that an atmosphere was prevailing that was charged with fear and doubt, which could be exploited with relative ease. All sorts of terrorist groups and antisocial elements could get maximum impact with relatively little effort. The presupposition that 'international terrorism' was *outside*, and the undiscerning and wide sweep of the term, meant that such incidents would be retrospectively constructed in a fashion that might have nothing to do with the reality behind them. The allocation of blame would under these circumstances depend on associations (most probably outside legal processes) with other allegedly guilty parties: there has, in short, seldom been a time when any perpetrators *as* perpetrators of specific terrorist acts are more likely to fade away behind the breadth of 'international terrorism' and the immediate enemy (bin Laden and al-Quaeda) in the Arab world. All that any terrorist group or antisocial element had to do was to let these associations flourish by not claiming responsibility – by allowing them to be seen as acts of silent terrorism which could feed into the environment created by the more devastating act of silent terrorism on 11 September. Irrespective of how globalised or not 'international terrorism' had been before 11 September, after that date an environment had been created, and the term 'international terrorism' had acquired a potency, that ensured that any act of terrorism could, with a little imagination, be given global effect. Ironically, the terrorist attacks of 11 September and the responses to them gave 'international terrorism' an air of reality and consequently an exploitable potential which it probably did not have before. There has also, however, emerged the contrary possibility: those political alignments that have engaged in terrorist activity of some sort till recently and may well have come under the aegis of 'international terrorism' with its current connotations might find the current environment suitable for making an emphatic statement of dissociation from 'international terrorism'. The IRA's long-awaited decision to decommission arms (a matter of much agonising in the many disappointing peace talks between Republicans and Unionists in Northern Ireland over the last decade), which was reported on 23 October, was undoubtedly influenced by, and would be all the more effective because of, the prevailing environment after 11 September. With this gesture the IRA managed to wipe away their association with globalised 'international terrorism', which was in the process of being constructed (through media reports on IRA involvement with Colombian guerrilla groups) before 11 September. It would be interesting to see how far this gesture impinges on the militant activities of the IRA and splinter republican groups, and those of their equally violent Unionist counterparts.

So far in this chapter I have: one, elucidated some of the connotations of 'international terrorism' as an abstraction; two, enumerated the advantages and disadvantages arising from these connotations for those who were conducting the so-called 'war against international terrorism'; and three, enumerated the advantages and disadvantages for those who could be considered to be the targets of this so-called 'war against international terrorism'. The conduct of the 'war against international terrorism' in abstract – the conduct of the war of abstractions – depended on how and to what effect either party could capitalise on its own advantages and exploit the disadvantages of the other. The frame of the war of abstractions and the possibilities that lay within that frame were there for all to see, and that is broadly what I have outlined above.

The war of abstractions in the context of military action in Afghanistan following the 11 September attacks occurred within that frame and in terms of the available possibilities. That war of abstractions is likely to recur in analogous ways, but with adjusted terms, as the 'war against international terrorism' expands in scope (away from Afghanistan and outwards). These broad features of the 'war against international terrorism' in terms of abstractions, which have evolved and emerged in the context of military action in Afghanistan, are worth noting: I don't think it is possible at the time of writing to infer from these where the 'war against international terrorism' in terms of abstractions would eventually end.

Consequently I would like to take this discussion of the war of abstractions in a somewhat different direction: a closer examination of the war of abstractions at its most ephemeral *within* the West (the United States and Western Europe primarily) – within the collective consciousness of the West. My focus on the collective consciousness of the West should not be taken as suggesting that such ephemeral wars of abstraction do not prevail *outside* the West – in the Arab world – in the Middle East and elsewhere. My focus should be taken as being no more than an acknowledgement of the location and correlative discourses/languages through which these thoughts on 'international terrorism' after 11 September are unavoidably sieved, and within which the *insideness* and *outsideness* of any voice is problematically and, despite resistance and distaste, insurmountably constructed.

The most ephemeral level of the war of abstractions refers to the particularly baffling – yet especially effective because of that – arraignment of what could be thought of as *principles in abstract* in the Western perception and presentation of the 'war against international terrorism', which surfaces in a wide range of media commentaries, political statements, discussions in academic forums, cafés and cybercafés, offices, bars and in the streets. The confrontation of *principles in abstract* translates the complex network of the material and the theoretical, the practical and the ideological, in the 'war against international terrorism' into a Manichean struggle between two absolutely opposed normative positions, which in turn suggests a Manichean struggle between two absolutely opposed ethical positions ('good against evil'). The ethical positions are corollaries of the normative positions, and are generally untenable reductions of those normative positions, and as such are of little interest in themselves. The normative positions in question are themselves so far from being unambiguous and clear that to jump to the ethical positions which may be derived from them is to jump too far ahead. It is the normative positions that need to be interrogated in this context and within their own *principles-in-abstract* terminology.

If that preamble to this somewhat different focus appears unclear, I hope the naming of the *principles in abstract* that I have in mind will suffice to clear things up by their very familiarity: the 'war against international terrorism', those in the United States and the Western European countries have been given to understand, was and is a war for *democracy* against *terrorism* (and *fanaticism*). These are the normative positions, it seems, that have to be chosen between: *democracy* and *terrorism* (which is associated with *fanaticism*). Clearly not much of a choice when presented in that stark fashion. The ethical characterisations crowd behind those terms if they are taken on the grounds of their impressionistic surface-effect and not interrogated further. Interrogation however dissolves the apparent clarity of these oppositions – and such interrogation it seems to me is a matter of urgency after 11 September.

The rhetoric which poses these oppositions of *principles in abstract* persuasively and with confidence after 11 September does so because there is a substantial history already of such rhetorical usage. It is not my intention to delve into that history in an academic spirit, but to highlight some characteristic instances of this in some relatively well-considered contexts (I confine myself, as I have before, to symptomatic academic presentations and examinations thereof). With ready glibness, that rhetorical opposition can be presented in an academic discussion of terrorism and democracy as matters of *principles in abstract* as follows:

> Democracy is rule by the majority while respecting the right of the minority. Terrorism is an instrument of rule of a tyrannic minority whether in or out of power. Democracy involves respect for rules when engaged in disputes and conflicts. Terrorism's strategy is based on transgressing rules of civilised conduct. Democracy involves tolerance of those who think differently. Terrorists are, in Marx's words, 'dangerous dreamers of the absolute'. These are some of the dichotomies that create problems for democratic societies.[7]

There are many incidental problems with this particular arraignment of oppositions. For example, what is the status of rule by a majority (which follows an elective process associated with democracy as majoritarian rule) which does *not* respect the right of the minority? Can terrorism be the instrument of a majority within a legislatively democratic government against an unpopular minority? Is it ever possible for a minority which takes recourse to terrorist acts justifiably *not* to regard the existing rules as being civilised (what absolute moral position does that morally loaded term derive from)? Does democracy's 'tolerance of those who think differently' exclude the 'dangerous dreamers of the absolute'? Can 'dangerous dreamers of the absolute' become a majority under certain circumstances and in certain contexts? Is it acceptable to find a dichotomy between democracy as *practice* (wherein a range of instruments may be utilised) to terrorism as an *instrument* (which may be used for a range of different practices)? Is it not the case that a dichotomy is being predetermined by defining democracy as an ideological principle with a certain ethical weight (civilised) and terrorism as its opposite (tyranny)? These questions arise out of an unconsidered obfuscation of two senses of 'democracy': democracy as a particular kind of practice (something like majority rule determined by some elective mechanism which subscribes to certain institutional processes and juridical strictures), and democracy as an ideological principle (something like government with the sanction of people in general and in the interest of the people in general – how integrity with regard to this sanction and protection of interests is maintained are procedural matters which may be debated, but the principle itself is unnegotiable and not correlative to a particular kind of practice). Now while it is possible and even likely that democracy as a particular kind of practice and democracy as ideological principle as described above might cohere, it is not *necessary* that they should. The questions that have been raised above arise out of the fissures that can exist between these conceptions of democracy as a particular kind of practice and democracy as ideological principle. The positing of terrorism – with the instrumentalist inflection of the above quotation – as being incompatible with democracy as practice or democracy as ideological principle becomes questionable because it can seep into those fissures. Under certain circumstances democratic practice may be adhered to and yet the ideological principle of democracy may be contravened, or alternatively it is conceivable that the ideological principle of democracy may be adhered to and yet the ostensibly democratic practice may be subverted. It is in the midst of these fissures that terrorism in an instrumental sense (as in the above quotation) may be inserted into an ostensibly democratic practice or under the aegis of an apparently sound democratic ideological principle. It seems to me that the incompatibility of democracy and terrorism is best argued for if one confines oneself to thinking about democracy either as practice or as ideological principle. This is a matter I come to in due course.

A more serious problem with the above quotation (and that kind of argument generally) from our post-11-September perspective of 'international terrorism' is that it assumes that terrorism (linked to tyranny) and democracy are both to do with territorial control, and as such are incompatible modes of territorial control. Both are with regard to government and affect those who are governed; the two therefore are incompatible insofar as they are manifested *within* a territory and with regard to a discrete people who are to be ruled. In the context, however, of 'international terrorism' as understood after 11 September – which always comes from *outside* – it is entirely unclear whether territorial control and contestations with regard to government *within* are the issues and it has certainly been widely assumed that they are not. On the whole the consensus is that 'international terrorism' as understood after 11 September is most closely associated with territorial influences and contestations of influence exerted *outwards* from certain political states and alignments with regard to other political states and alignments – as manifested within the realm of international politics. The fallout of the 'war against international terrorism' within the domestic front in the West (in terms of the sanctioning of xenophobia and racism, in terms of the curtailment of civil liberties, etc.) is a peripheral matter; the centre of the war is in the arena of international politics, which Kenneth Waltz had influentially described as a zone of anarchy, of the *realpolitik*.[8] Waltz's views on the competitive role of political states on the international stage and the consequent anarchy that arises from this had been hotly contested by a range of international relations theorists, and with substantial grounds: some accused him of overlooking, for instance, the regulatory role that international law and regulatory bodies play, or that economic and political unilateral and multilateral interstate alliances and agreements may provide; others felt that he was offering universalistic and ahistorical formulations which actually have no more than limited efficacy.[9] I am not sure whether one may regard Waltz's formulations as being permanently undermined, but it does seem to me that the events of 11 September, and the 'war against international terrorism' in abstract that has followed, have reinvigorated the spirit of Waltz's characterisation of international relations. 'International terrorism' is that factor (which Waltz had not taken into account) which is pervasive and *outside* and which reinserts the spirit of anarchic competitiveness and ruthless *realpolitik* that characterised international politics for Waltz. But what is the status of the opposition of democracy and terrorism as *principles in abstract* in this field of anarchy? The answer to that question has to be postponed until the relative merits of presenting the opposition of democracy as practice to terrorism and the opposition of democracy as ideological principle to terrorism are clarified and distinguished.

A relatively focused effort to work out the incompatibility of terrorism in an instrumentalist sense (more broadly characterised as 'political violence') with democracy as practice appeared in Ted Honderich's *Three Essays on Political Violence* (1976) (nothing as coherent and focused has appeared since as far as I am aware). In this he presents: (a) a characterisation of political violence as a particular sort of intervention within political practices of different sorts; (b) a characterisation of democracy as political practice which meticulously tries to find terms that accommodate the maximum number of conceivable variations in the implementation of that practice, and are (as far as possible) free of ethically loaded inflections; and (c) a careful argument against trying to find incompatibility between political violence and democracy as ideological principle. Whether Honderich was successful in these arguments is not my present concern – his conclusion of the ways in which *political violence could be considered to be incompatible with democracy as practice* is best given in his own words:

Guided by our findings about political violence and systems, we can conclude about political violence that it breaks the rule of democracy that electors and candidates are not to be coerced, and also the rule that each citizen is to have one vote, where that is understood to require equal participation in a fundamental procedure which gives rise to political decisions. Violence may be said to break the latter rule because the relative efficiency of the procedures is reduced. Thirdly, violence may be said to break the rule of democracy that each citizen is to have an approximately equal role in the influencing of governments, where what is in question is something other than voting. Fourthly, violence breaks the rule of democracy that governmental decisions are to be taken as binding, that the rule of law is to prevail.

We thus have a clear conflict between violence and democracy. Violence breaks rules of the practice.[10]

Insofar as we accept that the rules of democracy as practice are such as Honderich says they are, and insofar as there is no untoward interference from notions of democracy as ideological principle, and insofar as these rules of democracy are understood not to contradict each other under specific circumstances, Honderich's demonstration of the incompatibility of democracy with political violence (and therefore naturally with terrorism) can be considered a sound one. What is also clarified through a consideration of Honderich's argument is that this particular demonstration of the opposition of democracy and terrorism doesn't apply to the situation that obtains from the terrorist attacks of 11 September – the 'war against international terrorism' in abstract, the war of abstractions. That is because Honderich's understanding of democracy in practice is still necessarily *within* a discrete territory and its polity – democracy in practice has to exist where rules of democracy such as those enumerated by Honderich are constitutionally enjoined on the state with regard to the territory and polity it is with regard to. In the field of international politics, where 'international politics' has emphatically edged itself since 11 September to unleash a Waltzian sense of anarchy and *realpolitik*, the Honderich-like apprehension of democracy as practice has no place.

My demonstration that Honderich's arguments do not apply to the Manichean conflict of *principles in abstract*, democracy v. terrorism, after 11 September may seem to be no more than a nicety. It was, I believe, instinctively obvious from the beginning that the traditional argument of the incompatibility of democracy in practice with terrorism would not apply here. But the clarification, even if just a bit too perspicacious, is useful, especially where so much of the rhetoric has been designed to blur distinctions and make things unclear. In the spirit of clarity therefore let me make the other obvious inference: *if* what is presented as a struggle between democracy and terrorism that commenced on 11 September is to make any sense, it *might* do so insofar as democracy is understood as an ideological principle. Without complicating this matter any further let me simply stick with the common-sense elaboration that I have used above of democracy as ideological principle: government with the sanction of people in general and in the interest of the people in general – how integrity is maintained with regard to this sanction and protection of interests is a procedural matter which may be debated, but the principle itself is unnegotiable and not correlative to a particular kind of practice. This is consistent enough with extant conceptual considerations of democracy as ideological principle, but it still won't do. It still has too much of an air of being concerned with a discrete territory and polity, with government and people *within* – but can it be extended to the field of international politics where the 'war against international terrorism' is waged?

There are two ways in which democracy as ideological principle might extend outside a discrete polity and territory to the sphere of international politics at large. For this to be the case, there would have to be a conscious and principled adherence to a democratic *perspective* that:

1. acknowledges the equality of *all* people of the world *insofar* as they are political subjects and political agents in any sphere of political, social or economic action with international (or transnational) effect that impinges upon them or that they choose to involve themselves in;
2. accepts the sovereignty of all political states that are in place as representing a discrete territory or polity (however that position may have been achieved) and are understood to be so by the people under their jurisdiction and by other political states.

These principles, or principles such as these, could be regarded as constituting democracy as ideological principle with regard to a sphere of international politics. It is obvious that these are broad statements of principle which would have to be qualified and extended in all sorts of ways to ensure that they were maintained in the practice of international politics. Justifiable conditions of departure from these principles might well have to be set out in the field of practice, but only insofar as these principles are thereby maintained. It is quite possible that under certain conditions the two ways enumerated here in which democracy as ideological principle in international politics could be maintained might contradict each other. It is possible, for instance, that international communities could be created with international memberships that gives extra privileges in determining courses of political and economic action to those within the communities than to those outside them (this is analogous to the citizens of a particular political state being given extra privileges in determining the conduct of that state compared to someone who is not a citizen). It can conceivably be the case that the sovereignty of a political state might not be recognised by other political states though it might be accepted by the polity in question, or vice versa. It is possible to argue that certain courses of politically effective action (such as, say, being involved in an international crime syndicate) might constitute sufficient grounds for the exclusion of those involved in that action from the perspective that extends democracy as ideological principle. There could be several other practical considerations and contexts that might require that qualifications and emendations and appendices be added to support the above-stated positions of democracy as ideological principle in international politics.

What is more important in this context though is not what may be considered to be permissible to maintain this principle, but what is not permissible because it undermines the principle in itself. Attention is drawn to one tricky issue in this area in a recent essay by William Bain, which discusses the possibility that a political state's commitment to democracy as practice within its polity and territory may contradict its commitment to democracy as ideological principle in international politics.[11] Bain presents this in terms of a conflict between an ostensibly democratic political state's duty to provide 'national security' arising from its commitment to democracy in practice within its territory and polity, and its duty to contribute to 'human security' at an international level arising from its commitment to democracy as ideological principle with international political effect. Bain mostly concerns himself with the consideration of problems raised by other political states which do not subscribe to a commitment to democracy as ideological principle, and how far a political state which does should extend its democratic perspective to the people who happen to be under the aegis of a political state that doesn't – and reaches the conclusion that there is 'no necessary reason to believe that [national security and human security] should always coexist in perfect harmony'.[12] This diplomatic and inconclusive conclusion however seems to me to be too easy: I am not convinced that this asymmetry should simply be accepted without demur. At the least, it seems to me that strong conditions can be reasonably attached as to when national security could be considered to take precedence over human security (or democracy as practice over democracy as ideological principle), and vice versa. *There is a strong case for maintaining that national security cannot take precedence over human security such that it comes to be perceived that some minority of people are arbitrarily more privileged as political subjects and agents than others (just by dint of the fact that they happen to have been born in or to live in a particular place).* That would destroy democracy as ideological principle not only with international effect but also *within* – it could give rise to the imperialist and fascist psyche of being chosen people *within* and ultimately defeat the functioning of democratic practice itself. It would almost inevitably be unjustifiable from any utilitarian point of view that can claim to understand humanness and be with regard to humanity. It would certainly contradict any claim to a moral commitment to humaneness. *National security cannot be defended at the expense of human security such that the principle of the sovereignty of political states is subverted without reasons which would be understood by those both within and without to be in the interest of democracy as ideological principle with international effect.* I don't think that contention needs much elaboration.

With those clarifications about what democracy as ideological principle with international effect consists in, it becomes possible to consider what its relationship is (how inevitably incompatible it is and why) with terrorism – and particularly 'international terrorism'. An act of loosely targeted political violence used as an instrument for asserting a political position and effectively declaring and commencing a state of war, that is undiscriminating about casualties (only wishing to cause maximum damage and suffering) across international borders and with international effect, is obviously entirely incompatible with democracy as political principle. As an act it both disregards the equality of people as political subjects and agents, and undermines the sovereignty of political states. That hardly needs to be stated. The question is why single out democracy as being especially opposed to terrorism? This description of an act of 'international terrorism' not only contradicts democracy as political principle with international effect, it contradicts any political principle with some sort of basis in rationality and some sort of potential for practice. It is certainly incompatible with socialism as ideological principle (even when espoused by a single-party government), and with theocracy as ideological principle (even when championed by a clerisy-centred government); it would probably be opposed to benevolent dictatorship if laid out as an ideological principle. I do not intend to devote space to arguing these points in detail as I have with democracy as ideological principle. That would be an unnecessary digression: I think it is reasonably clear to anyone who tries to work out any coherent ideological position and extend it to an arena of international politics that an act of 'international terrorism' as described above – as seen on 11 September – has no place in it. That is why, of course, such a degree of unanimity was expressed about the 'war against international terrorism' in abstract from such a wide range of ideologically differently oriented states. So, in what way is terrorism – especially as connoted in 'international terrorism' – a particular affront to democracy as ideological principle with international effect?

The answer sadly lies not in democracy as ideological principle and the surrounding rationalisations, but in those who espouse a democratic perspective in that spirit. An act of terrorism pushes those who are in a position to espouse such a democratic perspective to contradict themselves, to become instruments and co-extensions of that act of terrorism. There is an immense body of research into how terrorism makes the ostensibly democratic political state contradict its functioning in terms of democracy as practice – by curtailing civil rights, and introducing repressive legislation, and ceding increasingly authoritarian powers to policing and military institutions, etc. In the context of 'international terrorism' after 11 September, more thought needs to be given to the manner in which those political states which are in a position to exercise a democratic perspective (in terms of democracy as ideological principle) with international effect, contradict themselves, subvert their own *raison d'être*, and become instrumental in 'international terrorism' themselves. This is where the 'war against international terrorism' brings the two wars together – the war of abstractions and the war as military action. This is also where the war of abstractions, the 'war against international terrorism' in abstractions, departs most decisively from the war as military action. But in saying that, I am anticipating the next chapter; with regard to the Manichean struggle between democracy and terrorism as it is constructed within the Western perspective after 11 September, the above I think gives some sense of the ambiguities and complexities and indecisions and obfuscations entailed. In summary, I have merely extended ideas that have long been received wisdom to fit the connotations of 'international terrorism' as they have evolved since 11 September, and the international political motivations that have been exercised since 11 September – received wisdom that was succinctly given, for instance, by Ronald D. Crelinsten in 1990:

> Terrorism poses a threat to democracy not only by virtue of the violent acts directed against specific targets, but also and more importantly by virtue of the response that such acts evoke. The

best short-term antidote to terrorism 'from below' is terrorism 'from above'; the most effective way for a state to combat terrorism, at least in the short term, is through ruthless repression which disregards the rule of law or subjugates it entirely to the needs of national security. [...]

In a democracy, however, the state's monopoly on violence is usually severely constrained by the rule of law and the prerogatives of due process.[13]

Again, Crelinsten was speaking with an assumption of *internal* or domestic terrorism. As observed above, when it comes to 'international terrorism' as manifested on 11 September, the status of the rule of law and the prerogatives of due process are altogether vaguer. One cannot depend here on democracy as practice, but on the espousal of democracy as ideological principle with international effect, and therefore on the choices that are made by those who make such an espousal.

Following a related but distinct issue, the confrontation of democracy and terrorism since 11 September has been given a particular turn by the association of the latter with another term – *fanaticism*. It is not just that any kind of terrorism is constructed as being particularly opposed to democracy, but that since 11 September the connotations of 'international terrorism' have become indelibly associated with the definitive irrationality of fanaticism, and therefore democracy becomes the oppositional position which claims, by implication, *all* rationalism. Apart from the above discernment of democracy as a matter of practice and a matter of ideological principle, there are of course specific vested interests at play in this oppositional construction. It is no secret that when Bush or Blair or others talk about defending democracy – or more aptly 'our Western democracy' – they are actually talking about democracy neither as practice nor as ideological principle in the broadly theoretical senses above, but about the conjunction of associations between what passes for Western liberal democracy and corporate capitalism. In positing the definitively irrational fanaticism as the *other* of 'our Western liberal democracy' a certain appropriation of rationalism occurs in favour of the latter – the latter appears to become definitively rational just as the former is definitively irrational. I have examined elsewhere[14] the mendacity of such claims of rationalism in Western liberal democracy in collusion with contemporary corporate capitalism, and presented arguments demonstrating that there is only a very tenuous connection between democracy (in any sense) and the organisation of contemporary corporate capitalism, and do not intend to go into this at present. Such doubts have often enough been presented in sophisticated ways (and usually, contrary to popular misconceptions, without thereby promoting a classical Marxist ideology) from the perspective of economics, politics, sociology and cultural studies since the end of the Cold War. This is not of particular interest in the current context – but the operation of vested interests in associating 'international terrorism' with definitively irrational fanaticism *against* 'our Western liberal democracy' is worth noting in passing.

There are two points to be made in this connection which are of immediate interest in this context: one, I need to clarify in what way fanaticism is thought of as definitively irrational; and two, I need to examine whether there is a necessary connection between acts of 'international terrorism' such as those of 11 September – or indeed between the connotations that 'international terrorism' has acquired since 11 September – and what may be understood as fanaticism.

As far as understanding what fanaticism suggests, R.M. Hare's view that 'the roots of fanaticism lie in intuitionism and in the refusal or inability to think critically',[15] is sufficiently indicative of generally accepted perceptions. Fanaticism arises when a position (whatever it might be, it may be moral or political or religious), which appears to be more than simply a matter of individual eccentricity (it is a *position* of some sort, not a quirk), is energetically and single-mindedly maintained and promoted without any attempt to validate or rationalise or analyse it. The position that is so maintained and promoted may or may not be amenable to critical analysis (it is not necessarily in itself irrational), but this particular *mode* of maintaining or promoting it is irrational. Like many who have considered the nuances of fanaticism, Hare was primarily concerned with trying to determine how such fanaticism comes about, and made a useful distinction between the *impure fanatic* (a person who resorts to a fanatical espousal of positions because of his innate inability to think critically) and the *pure fanatic* (one who resorts to a fanatical espousal of positions not for lack of ability but out of some sort of perverseness). The latter, I think, is the sort of fanatic who is popularly associated with acts of terrorism, and Hare's description of the *pure fanatic* is therefore a matter of specific interest here: 'This would be someone who was able and willing to think critically, but somehow survived the ordeal still holding moral opinions different from those of the utilitarian.'[16] What is interesting about this description is that Hare seems to believe that the *pure fanatic* is likely to be a moralist, and that any rational moral position is ultimately a utilitarian one. This arises largely from Hare's disagreements with philosophical accounts of morality which draw upon intuitionism; and this shows how such accounts of fanaticism as definitively irrational may fall into the trap of defining rationality too narrowly or monolithically. As a matter of philosophical rigour it is always worth examining precisely what rationalistic position irrationalism is being defined from. At any rate this description of the *pure fanatic* is closest in spirit to that of the fanatical terrorist for the following reasons: it explains the irrationality which Hare believed (in typically consequentialist fashion), and which is popularly believed, to attach to any terrorist act; and it allows for the ability to reason and organise which enables terrorists to perform often difficult acts of violence and subversion.

A slightly different inflection is given to the definitive irrationality of fanaticism when it is associated specifically with terrorism (something that Hare wasn't doing), and which is particularly relevant to the post-11-September understanding of 'international terrorism'. This is discerned in such descriptions of the relationship between fanaticism and terrorism as the following by Taylor and Ryan (1989):

> The fanatic often seems to have a clear view of the world from a particular perspective (but not necessarily a consistent perspective), usually closely allied to a view widely held by others, but lying at the extreme of the continuum. This particular view provides a base from which everything is interpreted, and which determines the fanatic's actions. This may not be unique to the fanatic; in a way, we all have elements of this, but we seem to often reserve the term fanatic to refer to extreme views of this kind held about moral, political or religious issues. A further important feature of the fanatic seems to be his unwillingness to compromise, and his disdain for other alternative views.[17]

Despite appearances, this is not too far from Hare's understanding of the definitive irrationality of the fanatic, but it carefully avoids the pitfall of defining irrationality from any particular assumption about what rationalism is. In fact that kind of narrowness is here attributed to the fanatic (a disdain for alternative views and the single-minded espousal of a particular perspective). But irrationality is still definitively fanatical – only it is not irrationality as contrasted with a particular understanding of what is rational, but irrationality as *lack of balance* or *extremism*. To be unbalanced is popularly understood as being mad; balance, synthesis, finding the golden mean, idealism tempered by pragmatism, theory controlled by practice, etc. are the stuff of reason. With this inflection, though, fanaticism apparently comes closer to the spirit of 'international terrorism' especially as understood after 11 September. The possibility that such an unbalanced espousal of a particular perspective need not be unrelated to a balanced espousal of such perspectives ('we all have elements of this') explains how those charged with such ghastly acts can still associate themselves (and with some success) with religious and political and moral ideologies that have wide currency somewhere (*outside* mainly). The extremity that cannot be normal – that is madness – explains how fanaticism can result in the sheer brutality of a terrorist act, particularly an act of 'international terrorism' that simply kills between 4,000 and 6,000 people without demur.

Despite the temptation to accept these explanations which connect a definitively irrational fanaticism to acts of 'international terrorism' as perpetrated on 11 September, I still feel – and especially with reference to the terrorist attacks of 11 September – that the above doesn't present a *necessary* connection between fanaticism and 'international terrorism'. It is a possible connection. It is actually even a charitable view of the matter. But there is an alternative: the kind of 'international terrorism' that manifested itself on 11 September could be the result of an utterly cynical and cold and brutal and self-serving terrorist logic. To elucidate this too I need to tie the threads of some of the conclusions reached in the consideration of the war of abstractions to a focused consideration of the war as military action – to finally unite the two senses of war which actually constitute the 'war against international terrorism' that was declared and commenced by the terrorist attacks of 11 September.

5   'War Against International Terrorism' as Military Action

Every sane person should be afraid of the likely reaction – the one that has already been announced, the one that probably answers bin Laden's prayers. It is highly likely to escalate the cycle of violence, in the familiar way, but in this case on a far greater scale. The US has already demanded that Pakistan terminate the food and other supplies that are keeping at least some of the starving and suffering people of Afghanistan alive. If that demand is implemented, unknown numbers of people who have not the remotest connection to terrorism will die, possibly millions.

The US has demanded that Pakistan kill possibly millions of people who are themselves victims of the Taliban. This has nothing to do even with revenge. It is at a far lower moral level even than that. The significance is heightened by the fact that this is mentioned in passing, with no comment, and probably will hardly be noticed. I think we can be reasonably confident that if the American population had the slightest idea of what is being done in their name, they would be utterly appalled.[1]

That was Noam Chomsky's response on being asked whether he was afraid of what the United States's answer might be to the terrorist attacks of 11 September, shortly before the bombing of Afghanistan began. Noam Chomsky did not figure much in the media immediately after 11 September, except to be reviled in the United States media in a rejuvenated spirit of blind jingoism. But apart from the occasional word of abuse, silence was better for his critics, because Chomsky's views on United States foreign policy since the Second World War, his recognition that the United States (ably supported by Britain) has been the direct and indirect perpetrator or supporter of the greatest amount of international state terrorism and human rights abuse across South America, the Middle East and South-East Asia, and a range of countries in Africa – disguised by careful media manipulation and propaganda to make the United States appear (ironically) to be the chief exponent of democracy as ideological principle with international effect – is supported by careful documentation and research, presented in a series of books that have appeared regularly since 1969.[2] His conclusions are based on such careful research and lucid analysis that it is difficult to doubt that he knows what he is talking about when it comes to United States foreign policy. But such an understanding of the role of the United States in world affairs is not confined to Chomsky – others have found corroborative and supporting evidence along similar lines.[3] It is clear to all who examine the evidence that, as apparently the main exponent of democracy as ideological principle with international effect, the United States (and its staunch satellite in Europe, the United Kingdom) has an indifferent record. The United States's espousal of the cause of democracy as ideological principle has generally been a means and a cover for extending a politics of force in support of strategic and economic self-interest (or the interest of the capitalist corporations on which her economy relies).

It is Chomsky's understanding, and that of others who have examined the evidence, that the United States has usually been the *initiator* of state terrorism with international effect in the name of espousing the cause of democracy as ideological principle with international effect, generally at her own initiative and with her own interests at heart. When the United States has adopted counter-terrorist measures as a result of 'international terrorist' attacks against herself – especially since 1986 – this has usefully fed into the general policy of international state terrorism that she was already following. The United States has so much experience of perpetrating state terrorism and sponsoring state terrorism with international effect, while maintaining an apparent role of promoting democracy as ideological principle with international effect, that a certain routinisation of procedure has taken place – an examination of historical precedent allows us to make, with little difficulty, a reasonable prediction of how the United States will deploy military action, initiate a propaganda drive, and bully other nations into collaboration or support, or at the least silence, when needed. The United Kingdom has so much experience of aiding and abetting and gaining from such moves that her role in such situations is also entirely predictable. Noam Chomsky, in the inteview quoted above, made an informed prediction about how the United States was likely to respond to the terrorist attacks of 11 September. The Afghan holocaust that Chomsky bitterly envisioned might not quite have taken place, but the strategy that the United States and Britain was expected to follow has routinely been followed. But there is a difference this time. Chomsky hints at it: 'the [United States reaction] that probably answers bin Laden's prayers'. In this case the United States was not the *initiator* of state terrorism with international effect. In this case the United States's state terrorism – synonymous now with counterterrorist war, 'terrorism from above', 'war against international terrorism' as military action – has been made *instrumental*, it can be reasonably suspected, in 'international terrorism'. Whether the United States – and, always, Britain – would be able to turn the whole series of events that she has routinely set into motion after 11 September to her advantage with her usual panache remains a moot issue; the *instrumentalisation* of United States's state terrorism by 'international terrorism' is matter for serious concern.

The year 2001, judging from such information as is in the public domain, was until 11 September a year in which the United States had been unwilling to expand the scope of her international power politics in a militaristic fashion. Her Asian interests had never been so secure since the end of the Cold War. Though Ariel Sharon was a more intractable factor in the most enduring and controversial of friendships, and the string of Hamas terrorist attacks and Israeli military atrocities and assassinations was steadily making the regional situation worse, there was no reason from the United States's point of view for the status quo not to last somewhat longer. The need to placate the Arab world since 11 September had momentarily taken the United States–Israel relation to an unprecedented low that the United States couldn't have anticipated. The suffering of the Iraqi people under economic sanctions had been so prolonged that the media and media consumers were beginning to lose interest in it. Meanwhile the United States was quietly assured that Saudi Arabia could be depended on, and Iran (in a mood for liberalisation) had never seemed as amenable to friendly overtures since the Islamic revolution. The tacitly Hindu communal government of India and the recently imposed military dictatorship in Pakistan, having done their mutually threatening nuclear testing, and having endured (without too much worry) the resulting economic sanctions, were both especially keen to get along with the United States. Since Pakistan was the only country with influence on the Taliban, the United States could probably have counted on an indirect hold on the Taliban herself (the key position of Pakistan in this context has been amply demonstrated since 11 September). China had recently been invited to join the World Trade Organisation, and diplomatic relations with the United States had never been better, despite hiccups (the inexplicable error of bombing the Chinese Embassy in Belgrade during NATO air strikes against Serbia, or the mysterious affair of a USAF aircraft crashing into a Chinese one in Chinese airspace, or the embarrassing investigation of a Chinese academic in the United States on suspicions of spying which proved to be unfounded). The dark horse President Putin of Russia was busy handling the domestic situation and was inclined to be friendly. At any rate neither Russia nor China had shown any inclination to disturb United States interests in the Middle East. There was no significant oil shortage that would force the United States to contemplate dipping into her enormous oil reserves or to bully the Arabic countries first – nothing at any rate that couldn't be resolved by slow politics and diplomacy. The United States had plenty of opportunity to concentrate on her beloved, very expensive and entirely mindless Missile Defence Programme: that appears to have gained in credibility since 11 September, but there was no serious opposition to it before (bar a few faint mutterings from Western Europe and Russia). An eccentric spate of antiglobalisation protests seemed to be the only thing that the West in general had to worry about (that, it seems, has been effectively silenced by the events of 11 September).

The United States's response to the terrorist attacks of 11 September was however entirely predictable. The military action against bin Laden and the Taliban, and most materially against the people of Afghanistan, which may yet be extended to Iraq and other alleged harbourers of 'international terrorism' *out there*, was widely anticipated. Clearly, the United States was simply going through motions and routines long ingrained by the experience of *initiating* state terrorism. But this time the United States is not the *initiator*, this time the United States has simply gone mechanically and with clockwork-like predictability into its well-worn routine at the prodding of an *outside* hand – the perpetrators of the terrorist attacks of 11 September. It is possible that eventually the United States will be able to resist its well-ingrained tendency to depend on state terrorism with international effect, and so avoid causing more suffering to already suffering people. It is quite possible that changing domestic and international opinions may pressure her into doing so. It is perhaps possible that the United States may be able to turn the whole situation to her advantage and extend even stronger tentacles into the Middle East towards that precious oil. There is no doubt that the United Nations will continue to carry out mopping up operations (that too is part of the routine) after the United States finishes another tired demonstration of state terrorism with international effect. Tony Blair and his ministers had already been talking about the need to rebuild Afghanistan before it was reported on 25 October that the United States had reached an agreement with the United Nations whereby bombing of Afghanistan would be kept at a low level (low enough not to let the Northern Alliance occupy Kabul) while the United Nations puts together a transitional plan for government in Afghanistan after the Taliban (overcoming the Taliban, it is now understood, is what the first phase of the 'war against international terrorism' as military action was always meant to achieve). There is absolutely no doubt that any scepticism about this routine will be routinely answered by charging the sceptics with the appeasement of 'international terrorism' and by comparing them with Nazi appeasers (a bit of name-calling usually helps). But there is no getting away from this: the United States's penchant for state terrorism with international effect, for unleashing military forces on slight pretexts to serve deep self-interests in the name of democracy, has been *used in an instrumental fashion* by the perpetrators of the terrorist attacks of 11 September – and has become the terrible extension and product of that appalling act of 'international terrorism'.

Bin Laden's prayers have been answered. It is impossible that those who planned the terrorist attacks of 11 September, especially given the deliberateness with which the context was chosen and the scale of casualties which was targeted, would not have included the reaction of the United States and her allies within their calculations. It is impossible that they would not have been aware of the United States's penchant for military aggression, usually at her own initiative and for her own interests, and generally using far smaller provocation than these attacks; it is impossible that they wouldn't have known exactly what sort of specific and abstract targets would emerge if responsibility wasn't claimed and the United States and Western Europe were left to their own interpretations; it is impossible that they wouldn't have anticipated the kinds of polar-isation (xenophobic and racist) that were likely to occur within the West, and more importantly the kinds of polarisation and conflicts that were almost sure to occur within the Middle East. It is therefore certain that it was precisely this response that the terrorist attacks of 11 September were designed to provoke: the declaration and com-mencement of war on 11 September *sought* the initiation of the 'war against international terrorism' exactly along the lines that have since been followed.

But to what end has this instrumentalisation of United States's state terrorism been effected? Contemplation of the predictable manner in which the 'war against international terrorism' has so far unfolded and of the possible long-term consequences that have been evident from the beginning can lead to certain hypothetical answers – answers that are, I think, plausible and therefore impossible to dismiss out of hand. There is a cold and utterly brutal terrorist logic here that was designed to make the United States's ingrained state terrorism with international effect visible in all its sophisticated barbarity either *as an end in itself*, or as a deliberate means of creating polarisation within the West and destabilisation within the Middle East. It seems to me that both these calculations were probably at work, and that the expectations of terrorist logic are likely to be realised by the 'war against international terrorism' that the United States and allies have begun.

The perpetrators of the 11 September terrorist attacks in the United States were not religious fanatics in the sense of being persons who are consumed with religious hatred against those whom they consider to be heretics and religious determination to further the interests of those whom they consider to be kindred spirits. They cannot be considered Islamic fanatics in this mould because the fact that their attacks were designed to provoke the 'war against international terrorism', the war of abstractions and the military action that has been witnessed since, makes them the worst enemies of Muslims around the world and of the Islamic faith that history has seen. The perpetrators (in undertaking the 11 September attack with its predictable outcome in view), bin Laden and al-Quaeda (in having exploited every political association possible to turn this into a war of religions and cultures) and the demagogic Islamic clerics (who have taken bin Laden at his word and urged others to do the same) are the most vicious enemies of Muslims everywhere. To them, Muslim lives are as cheap as, and perhaps cheaper than, the lives of those who died in the World Trade Center on 11 September. By deliberately and calculatedly unleashing United States's state terrorism (a remorseless weapon) for their own purposes they have ensured that vast numbers of Muslims will be led to the slaughter like cattle. The killings of 11 September were intended only to ensure that the United States and its allies would kill ordinary Muslims in equal and greater numbers as a result – the perpetrators undoubtedly banked on their shared perception with the West of the cheapness of Muslim life. That the perpetrators regarded human life in a cavalier fashion, and the lives of gullible Muslims as being particularly expendable, is amply evidenced in the 11 September attacks themselves. Those doomed faces of the suicidal hijackers are the visages of victims too: the outer shells of brainwashed almost insentient beings, who have somehow been made to surrender their humanity and consciousness to become pure instruments of death, no less *things* than missiles or bombs. Such a surrender of the self is a murder committed before the vital signs give way, a withdrawal of life that denies even the dignity of natural death. It shows a contempt for that person's life – his conscience, his life and loves, his faith – that is more complete than for the victims who die at his hand. The victims are at least victims, they are dead *people*, but the instrument is someone whose very human essence has been sucked away and who can therefore be neither a victim nor a killer, only a cog. That this is done in the name of a faith can only be regarded as contempt for those who profess that faith, and especially those who surrender themselves to that faith without a sense of their humanity.

Polarisation that manifests itself in the unthinking popular imagination and in the protective institutional processes of the West as xenophobia and racism directed at the Arab world, and destabilisation within the Middle East that sees the bridges to the West crumbling and throws the priorities of the pragmatic states therein against their theocratic credentials, vitalising the medieval imagining of and longing for a religious war – these polarisations and destabilisations must be what the perpetrators sought. For those who thrive on warfare and strife and know little else, the condition of war is an affirmation of their existence and aspirations. That might sound like an impressionistic thought, presented in a somewhat rhetorical way – but what are bin Laden and al-Quaeda without conflicts and wars to fight? In the midst of wars they can hope to grow larger than themselves, become demons or heroes, exercise an awesome power over life and death without discrimination, enter into the stuff of myths – get *recognised*. Fukuyama influentially and controversially erected an argument in favour of corporate capitalist liberal democracy on the grounds of the universality of *recognition* as an ambition,[4] and when he did so some recognised in his conservative argument something like the zeal of a preacher.[5] Not dissimilarly but of a different order, behind the ostentatious religious zeal of a bin Laden there probably lies a brutal drive for *recognition*. A drive for recognition seeks to create the conditions wherein that drive can find its fulfilment. When the terrorist attacks of 11 September led inexorably to the 'war against international terrorism', through which the United States and her allies were able to fall into a well-rehearsed routine of state terrorism with international effect, bin Laden's prayers were answered.

Through the declaration and commencement of war on 11 September bin Laden has conquered the mind of the West. He has absorbed the whole fantasy and dread of the Arab world that exists most potently in the social psyche of the West into his image.

But what else could the United States and her Western allies have done after 11 September? There are several sane answers that have been proposed in the media – but that is not my concern here. This book is not intended to find solutions that might have been, but to analyse what has been.

On 29 October in the Pakistani village of Bhowalpur gunmen entered a church and opened fire on the congregation, killing 30 people. The newspapers reported that a large number of Pakistani men had gathered their Kalashnikovs and were heading towards Afghanistan to join the holy war. It was also reported that some of the Muslim youth of Britain had found their way to Afghanistan to fight for the Taliban (though the family of one of the youths so named insisted that their son had gone to Afghanistan as an aid worker). Meanwhile the United States continued to drop bombs over Kabul and other cities, apparently taking out Taliban posts, but it was unclear what was being achieved by this. It was also becoming ever clearer that the 'surgical' operation was routinely killing civilians. Whatever spin one puts on this, the 'war against international terrorism' was metamorphosing into a religious war as was widely feared from the beginning. In spite of the clinical rhetoric of the United States and Britain and other allies, the features of a religious war had seeped through. It was clear that the single-mindedness of United States's state terrorism was not only instrumentally unleashed to drum up a religious war, but that the United States had in some sense accepted that instrumental role and given it full reign, had indeed taken the initiative even while being instrumental. On 27 October it was reported that George Bush had sanctioned the CIA to eliminate all suspected al-Quaeda cells anywhere, through 'covert operations'. 'Covert operation' can also, of course, be read as assassination. *Covert* means that judicial procedure and the processes of determining culpability have been suspended in a wider sense – not just bin Laden and al-Quaeda in Afghanistan but *anyone suspected of adhering to their ideology anywhere* can now be eliminated, neutralised, assassinated without further demur. At this point the abstraction of 'international terrorism' finds a sudden clarification in terms of military action: those who can be thought of as being adherents of an ideology of extremist Islam. Since the ideology of the *other side* ('international terrorism' from *outside*) has been thought of as extremist Islam all through – the irrationality of fanaticism rather than the callous logic of instrumentalisation and destabilisation – it is *that* ideology which has to be destroyed. But who is to determine what is fanatical and what isn't fanatical? Fanaticism is not a particularly clear identifier; being a Muslim and faithful to Islam regretably is. Bush's sanction to the CIA to assassinate the proponents of this 'fanatical' ideology inevitably becomes a sanction to attack anyone who actively promotes a puritanical Islamic ideology and who could always retrospectively be tagged as being 'fanatical'. But people *outside*, in the Arab world, would know better, and a religious war would be perceived as a duty from *out there*. The 'covert' war against a religious ideology will probably be an endless war – for when can one be sure that the ideology is dead? The most cold-blooded strategists in the United States had always known that if a war against a religious ideology is initiated it might well become a continuous war with no visible end. What such a war might mean from a Western point of view was envisaged by Sandler and Enders not too long before 11 September 2001:

> To provide security for all potential targets, a government must embark on proactive anti-terrorist campaigns to infiltrate terrorist groups or destroy their resource base. A religious or amorphous terrorist group must be annihilated completely. Destroying even a large portion of a group may not ameliorate the dangers for long, because remaining fanatical members may attack with even greater resolve and vengeance. Because some religious terrorist organizations are associated with extreme elements that splinter off, the threat posed by such groups may grow over time unless the group is neutralized.[6]

The terrifying resolve marked in this bit of mindless 'strategy speak' seems to lie behind Bush's sanction to the CIA to carry out 'covert operations'. The shape of a much feared religious war began to emerge from the shadows as October 2001 drew to an end.

A war that is understood to be against what is – irrespective of the attribution of fanaticism – ultimately a religious ideology can always be interpreted as being one that is conducted at the behest of a religious ideology (and just as grimly fanatical) too. That perception is all that matters.

It seems reasonably clear that through the labyrinth of abstractions and covert or overt military action, 'international terrorism' – which now *contains* and *instrumentalises* the United States's (and her Western allies') state terrorism with international effect – will continue to expand and spiral into a consuming whirlpool for some time to come.

Oxford, 1 November 2001

Postscript
Happenings and Unthinkingness

The attack on the World Trade Center is the first of the post-Cold War. No matter who is responsible, it ushers in a new era of terrorism having nothing in common with the explosions that regularly rock Ireland or England.

Indeed, the outstanding feature of the attack is that it was seriously intended to bring down the World Trade Center building; in other words, to bring about the deaths of tens of thousands of innocent people. [...] So it is not a matter of a simple remake of the film *Towering Inferno*, as the image-conscious media like to keep saying, but much more of a strategic event confirming for us all *the change in the military order of this fin-de-siécle*.

[...]

With the New York bomb, we thus find ourselves faced with the latest escalation in the kind of military-political action that is based simultaneously on a limited number of actors and guaranteed media coverage. It has reached the point where soon, if we don't look out, a single man may well be able to bring about disasters that were once, not long ago, the province of a naval or air force squadron.

Indeed, for some time the miniaturization of charges and advances in the chemistry of detonation have been promoting a previously unimaginable equation: One man = Total war.[1]

This was Paul Virilio's response of 30 March 1993 (it appears in *A Landscape of Events*, which is organised in dated sections as a kind of intellectual's diary for the period between November 1984 and May 1996 in reverse order) to the bomb explosion in the World Trade Center of 26 February 1993, in which six people died and over a thousand were injured. Eventually six conspirators were imprisoned for 240 years each for the crime.

What sort of feeling does this apparently prophetic statement arouse now that the worst case scenario imaginable of an attack on the World Trade Center has actually occurred? One might be struck by the veracity of this prediction: one might feel that Paul Virilio's provocative political and cultural readings have gained in persuasiveness, and that his reputation as someone who represents the cause of human justice and radical social change (and is happily acknowledged as such by those who espouse a liberal or left politics) has been confirmed. His admittedly eclectic but immensely suggestive pronouncements on the intensification of war and the military machine in the modern world; on the 'denaturing of science' and 'banalization of *cold perspective*'[2] brought about by science, which has turned into technoscience, devoted to increasing speed and fragmentation in the service of war; on the manner in which the development of mass media (which incorporates an acquisition of speed such that 'real-time' or 'live' broadcast grows numbingly pervasive and replaces the more comfortable pace of cinema)[3] both exposes and mediates a pervasive violence or comprehensive state of war in our world; on the manner in which technological developments marked by the deterrence principle have enabled '*a transfer of war from the actual to the virtual*';[4] on the processes through which every aspect of human existence and culture is taken over by a geotemporal concentration that disables political agency and accedes supremacy to the military machine and multinationals; on the decentring of this military machine through the same processes which make the inconceivable equation ('One man = Total war') realisable in the not-too-distant future; and so on – all these now familiar partly analytical, partly visionary and always rhetorically attractive positions taken by Virilio may now appear to have gained a character of eccentrically radical *truth*. Indeed post-11-September Virilio-like pronouncements are some of the few, amongst those that have for some time received the approbation of liberal and leftist sympathisers, which are likely to continue to receive general and indeed increased approbation in the future. The degree to which the tone of the above-quoted response to the 1993 World Trade Center bombing cohered with what was the dominant tone of those conducting the 'war against international terrorism' is ample evidence of that. Virilio-like thinking and position taking may well become the only kind of ostensibly liberal or left-leaning politics that will be tacitly tolerated hereafter and acknowledged as reliably liberal and left-leaning in Western institutional spaces (the others could by that dint be marked off as unacceptable, undemocratic, terrorist-friendly, etc., and effectively banished from any sort of institutional space) – if 'we' (and, as in the quotation above, I mean everybody) don't look out.

Regretfully, Virilio's consanguinity with dominant institutional thinking in the West, as well as the marginal liberal and left-leaning residual politics in the West, arises from a certain *unthinkingness*, covered by a persuasive veil of erudition and analytical verbiage intermingled with genuinely perceptive political and cultural observation. I use the coinage *unthinkingness* deliberately, as a quality that is not intrinsically mendacious and can coexist with a great deal of well-meaning and well-intentioned political passion. There is no doubt that Virilio's observations on the manifest patterns of technological development are often acute – observations on increasing degrees of speed in technology and the impact this has on the exertion of political power and political/cultural perspectives, on the manner in which these are played out through negotiations (or lack thereof) between virtual images and real happenings, of the dislocation and disappearance of political agency from traditionally familiar agents, of the increasing ubiquity of certain anxieties and conflicts, and so on. There is no point in dwelling on these observations; they are immediately familiar to all who are aware of Virilio's work. These often keen observations are just as often presented through analytical devices (I don't complain about the patchwork of disjointed erudition that Virilio uses) which are impressionistic, inconsistent, ultimately debilitatingly *unthinking* – *unthinking* with the effect of becoming endlessly appropriable and mistranslatable (especially into English, which matters since Anglophone imperialism is more widespread than Francophone imperialism). That is the reason, no doubt, why Virilio is amenable to a wide spectrum of convictions. Consider, for example, Virilio's preoccupation with understanding war – understanding war is a matter that I have discussed in Chapter 3. On consideration it becomes evident that in fact Virilio constantly pushes 'war' further and further into the a priori, such that with each push the perpetually a priori 'war' acquires another shade of effect (and by the same process accrues another shade of possible meaning) which is immediately emptied by pushing it again into another direction of being a priori. In this process, 'war' as a concept (if it could be thought of as anything so unitary for Virilio) seems to be both a perpetually *ultimate* as well as a perpetually *immediate* cause. In this process also, 'war' evades every effort at analytical *understanding* or engagement, it becomes something like a first cause and a constant cause which can only be *manifest* and *recognised* – it becomes mystical (there is a great deal of the mystical in Virilio's thinking). So, for Virilio, 'war' lies behind and leads on to the births of civilisation, collectivity and economics themselves, the gradual development of urban architecture and geographical and temporal apprehension; 'war' constantly lies behind and urges on technological development, the intensification of speed, the concentration and depletion of human ability and agency; and 'war' is also the immediate cause of, and is evidenced in, every malaise that seems to Virilio to afflict our world. 'War' is therefore only available through symptoms – like the abstractly institutional as well as the flesh-and-blood 'military', like all kinds of evident violence, like the voluntary and involuntary manifestations of strategy replaced by logistics, like the symbolic potency of any machine that has a spatial-temporal presence – which nevertheless do not lead to a diagnosis of 'war' (as a condition, concept, idea, state of affairs, or anything at all). Virilio's 'war' is constructed, or rather not constructed, to discourage analysis; or, in other words, Virilio's 'war' is the formulation of *unthinkingness*.

Not unsurprisingly 'war' for Virilio often comes with qualifiers that discourage interrogation – 'absolute war', 'total war', 'pure war'. In the early nineteen-seventies, when Raymond Aron wrote his assessment of the life, work and impact of Clausewitz, he observed that in the Cold War period the distinction between war and not-war, maintained by Clausewitz and the Marxist-Leninists, had been deliberately and untenably obfuscated in the United States.[5] Virilio's formulation of 'war' is a kind of logical progression from that Cold War obfuscation to a post-Cold War totalisation – so that there can be nothing but 'war'.

That sort of formulation can according to Virilio be extended to other areas of his thinking (unthinking?) – politics, technology, science, geography, etc. But there are other impediments to analysis in Virilio's work too. The confident glibness with which he offers ethical evaluations, or more often ethical inflections, is a substantial stumbling block to the thinker who hopes to be rigorous. Consideration of a statement such as the following, chosen more or less randomly, will serve to make the point:

> The banalization of *cold perception* – paradoxically, a privileged feature of the scientific gaze – in fact developed an aesthetics specific to that gaze: a kind of *elementary structuralism* which was to infuse fields as various as the visual arts, literature, industry,

design or even the social and economic utopias of the nineteenth and twentieth centuries.[6]

There is ethical disapproval here, mainly conveyed (in this translation) by the association of words: in 'banalization' (presumably of something exciting), in the 'paradoxical' privilege (as opposed to natural privilege), in the 'cold perception' (as opposed to an affectionately warm look), in the 'elementary structuralism' (suggesting something primitive compared, perhaps, to complex poststructuralism). The imputation of 'elementary structuralism' to *all* science (reminiscent of an equally *unthinkingly* judgemental Barthes)[7] is, I suspect, simply wrong. That an exciting, warm, complex, naturally privileged aesthetics (even if we know what that might mean) is ethically desirable needs a lot more demonstration and debate. As it stands, it is no more than an unthinking appeal to a certain culture-specific sentimentality. The ethical inflections that Virilio repeatedly loads on to his otherwise acute observations, with inadequate analysis, do those observations a disservice. No one can deny that speed is a useful concept, in a number of different ways, for understanding human social development and for coming to grips with the present, but if ethical disapproval attaches to the excessive speed of the contemporary world (related to the perception that 'speed is violence')[8] then the *desirable* or *natural* pace has to be indicated and justified as such. Virilio unthinkingly doesn't do that.

Finally, the *unthinkingness* of Virilio's work is contained in the rhetorical flourishes that he is so fond of. To express the observation that one man might in the future become capable of causing substantial destruction – might even destroy the world – as an equation of the form 'One man = Total war' is a case in point. Whatever semantic understanding one brings to it that equation remains unadulterated nonsense.

Let me go back to the quotation from Virilio's response to the 1993 bombing of the World Trade Center, which is likely after 11 September 2001 to be regarded as so astonishingly prescient. It is, to be blunt, a monument to the *unthinkingness* that characterises much of Virilio's work. I refer to the English translation, which is and will continue to be Virilio's main passport in the West and elsewhere. 'The attack on the World Trade Center is the *first* of the post-Cold War' [my italics], says Virilio. What could that mean? Where was that period of post-Cold War world peace when no attacks took place anywhere? What ideological location does the person who says that so confidently have to occupy? '[it is] a strategic event <u>confirming</u> for <u>us all</u> the change *in the military order of this fin-de-siécle'* [my under-lining], he continues. Who are the 'us all' who had suspected this 'change in the military order' all along? This manifests, he carries on, an 'escalation in the kind of military-political action' that could lead to a single individual causing destruction that was, 'not long ago, the province of a naval or air force squadron'. Is that inference really possible from the 1993 World Trade Center bombing? When could one locate clearly the monopoly of mass-destruction within the military, and the relative harmlessness of individuals? (The first time arson was conceived? the invention of gun-powder? or the cannon? or the machine gun? or dynamite? ...) At what point could one see the potential for individuals causing destruction to compete with an army in terms of capacity and technological development? And then, of course, there is that unfortunate 'equation'.

I don't think I need to answer those questions. Luckily, some of the ideological implications that would become manifest in trying to answer those questions are contradicted by numerous other statements that Virilio has made, and in more careful investigations that he has conducted elsewhere. It is the inconsistency of *unthink-ingness*; I have few doubts that Virilio is well intentioned in a liberal, perhaps even loosely socialist, fashion.

Much of the prodigious amount of discussion that has been and continues to be produced and publicly relayed about the political and cultural repercussions of the attacks on the World Trade Center on 11 September 2001 – especially in the United States and Britain – seems to me to be pervaded by *unthinkingness*. At best, when well intentioned and apparently erudite, when interrogative and prepared to challenge official pronouncements and perceptions if necessary, such discussion often takes forms not unlike Virilio's response to the 1993 World Trade Center bombing, with a Virilio-like sense of disenchantment with the contemporary world order. More often, such discussion is simply – obtusely – *unthinking*; and occasionally *unthinking* in an ill-judged or ill-advised or even delib-erately ill-intentioned manner. This would be impossible for me to demonstrate in a systematic fashion yet, so I won't try. But I am convinced it could be adequately demonstrated with more hindsight, when these discussions have been organised and collated and archived.

Though analytically *unthinking* himself, Virilio has well-honed sensibilities that enable him to observe *unthinkingness* around him in ways that are especially pertinent in the aftermath of 11 September 2001. I am reminded of sentiments expressed by him in a discussion with Sylvère Lotringer, published under the title *Pure War*, such as:

> All of us are already civilian soldiers, without knowing it. And some of us know it. The great stroke of luck for the military class's terrorism is that no one recognizes it. People don't recognize the militarized part of their identity, of their consciousness.[9]

Or

> [Lotringer] *Do you think that State terrorism, State delinquency, is the fragmentation of general war as we have known it in this century?*
> [Virilio] The general narrative of Total War has crumbled in favor of a fragmented war which doesn't speak its name, an intestinal war in the biological sense.[10]

Without trying to investigate what Virilio means by 'war' here, or what he specifically meant *when* he said this, and substituting instead what has been understood as war in Chapter 3 in the context of the 'war against international terrorism' after 11 September 2001, these sentiments seem to me to be especially relevant now. With the intensification that comes about in a perceived condition of war (following Wright, whom I have quoted in Chapter 3) there occurs an *internalisation* of the military in contexts where that war seems relevant, an 'intestinal war' appears in concert with the war without. No doubt this occurs because a – possibly latent – military aspect is instilled in all consciousnesses already, since people are acclimatised to the social world in different ways: but that psychosocial issue is not my concern. After 11 September in the United States, as in Britain and other parts of the West, an *unthinkingness* is pervasive, which doesn't seem to recognise its collusion in an instrumentalised state terrorism, which cannot wholly believe that an instrumentalisation of state terrorism can occur, and which doesn't wish to speak its name even if it knows it. The internalised military part of the prevailing social psyche of the United States and her allies is kept in order by the eagerness to avoid any accusation of having a terrorist part: the military and legislative apparatus of these states demands social consensus by coercing those who might not ultimately collude – dissent has now become indicative of a terrorist part in the psyche. Bush's 'either with us or with the terrorists' is the rallying slogan of this phenomenon, which keeps echoing and reverberating through the media, through all those unthinking discussions, in different ways. *Unthinking* rhetoric and formulations are what remain, because these provide an illusion of debate, of multiplicity, of erudite and scholarly engagement with ethical and humanitarian concern, even of dissent – but only because behind *unthinkingness* uncomfortable and immediate recognitions and doubts can be hidden away.

The prevailing comfort of *unthinkingness* makes theorising about the happening world a tricky matter, even with the conviction that theorising is contingent on the happening world and the happening world cannot, in the long run, perhaps even now, be indifferent to the perceptions that follow theorising (*thinkingness*). There is a well-known and well-established prejudice involved here. Isn't it rather obscene to be philosophical (or aesthetic for that matter) when something as urgent as a war is in progress, and people are dying, and momentous happenings are afoot? Shouldn't philosophy withdraw to a respectful distance into a future in which there is relative tranquility and from which retrospection on a violently happening past becomes possible? Impassioned advocacy, clear partisanship, rousing rhetoric are the *unthinking* intellectual engagements that are appropriate to the world that is intensely happening. This prejudice finds its way into the very structures and conventions of theorising – into thinking philosophy itself. Even as I record events which are unfolding about me and try to bring them into a political-philosophical perspective, the events seem to become historical and the thoughts retrospective as I set them down on the page. I am tempted to use the past tense to describe events, matters, environments, reflections that are all too present.

I cannot attempt to bring into a philosophical perspective that is in any conventional sense systematic events that are unfolding as I write, events which are *not* yet history. But I can attempt to bring into a philosophical perspective, which is not incoherent and not unthinking, events (and representations thereof) that are unfolding as I write by encountering such events almost randomly, by letting them float to the surface of this text – of my consciousness – as they occur, without a retrospectively imposed structure and apprehension. It might be that as I record and comment on these events and their representations, they seem to become historical, entrenched in a past by dint of my doing this, but that has happened already in the five preceding chapters. What follows is merely a brief sampling of this possibility; as a project such an attempt can have no end.

*On 3 November 2001 the Northern Alliance announced that it had
captured regions around the strategically important city of Mazar-e-Sharif.
By 9 November, after a period of intense fighting, the city was captured.
On 13 November it was announced on the media that Kabul had been
'liberated'. There was no significant opposition from the Taliban, most of
whom had vacated the city. Pictures in newspapers, television images,
showed the people of Kabul enjoying their new-found freedom – men
shaving off beards, women appearing in public (some even with their faces
uncovered), people watching television, shopping, and generally looking
cheerful. That itself, it was felt, vindicated the military campaign in
Afghanistan. Western governments, the media reported, were taken aback
by the speed with which the Taliban were giving in – instead of fighting
to the death like the brain-washed zombies they had been made out to be
earlier, it was found that Taliban soldiers were ready to retreat, defect or
surrender, as any group of sensible soldiers might. After a brief siege, on 7
December Kandahar, the stronghold of the Taliban and base of the
Taliban leader, Mullah Omar, surrendered to the Northern Alliance.
Mullah Omar, however, escaped. Meanwhile, it had become evident that
some sort of government needed to be established in the recently occupied
territories to replace the Taliban, and after some tough negotiations in
Bonn a power-sharing deal between the different Northern Alliance
factions was reached on 4 December. This however soon (reported on 6
December) threatened to fall apart as two important leaders of the
Northern Alliance, General Abdul Rashid Dostam of the Uzbek faction
and Ismail Khan, former governor of Herat, criticised the agreement and
threatened to boycott it. Over this period several massacres of cornered or
captured Taliban soldiers by the Northern Alliance were reported and the
American bombing continued. Northern Alliance and American troops
then advanced further south in Afghanistan, to the Tora Bora mountains
where Osama bin Laden was believed to be in hiding, and started a
prolonged bombing of the hills.*

The attacks on the Taliban and the occupation of Taliban-
controlled Afghanistan kept slipping through the grasp of both kinds
of the 'war against international terrorism'. The process of defeating
the Taliban, those who 'sponsored terrorism', didn't in its unfolding
meet the objectives of either the 'war against international terrorism'
as military action or the 'war against international terrorism' in
abstract. The war of abstractions could have had some sort of con-
sistency with the military action (despite the rift between them that
I have marked out in previous chapters) if the military action could
have demonstrated somehow that 'international terrorists' had been

overcome, that the perpetrators of 'international terrorism' had been punished. This could have been achieved to some degree if the Taliban had demonstrated, as they were expected to, some sort of collective terrorist psyche – that of unthinking irrational maniacal semi-automatons who lay down their lives (not unlike those who perpetrated the 11 September attacks) for their faith. (Many Hollywood films have ensured a suitable automatic response to this situation: it would have been as satisfying as John Wayne dealing with bad Red Indians or bad Vietnamese, Flash Gordon or Captain Kirk or Captain Picard sorting out bad aliens, or Chuck Norris single-handedly beating up bad Arabs in large numbers.) This patently did not occur. So predictably frail, under the circumstances, was the Taliban's response (as everyone in the West knew it would be, but had unthinkingly hoped it wouldn't so that the 'war against inter-national terrorism' could be understood as such) that it almost seemed as if the United States was, in its military action, not only fighting shadows but also using disproportionate force against what was real. A grim absurdity threatened to undermine the whole operation. Something of a success for 'the war against international terrorism' through military action could have been announced – and the media pictures of the happily 'liberated' in Afghanistan might have helped this – if any of it had been convincing. After all, the happiness of those 'liberated' from the tyranny of the Taliban (arguably, tyranny has been historically associated with terrorism) could mark the success of this phase of the 'war against international terrorism'. But this wasn't convincing. It rankled that this 'liberation' was suspect: 'liberation' *to* what? It was far from clear whether an unstable government of the Northern Alliance, which was then imminent, could be regarded as a welcome prospect. Historical precedent suggested that it couldn't be regarded as such. And over the smiling faces of those 'liberated' people of Kabul (and elsewhere) that featured in newspapers and on television, there hung – didn't there? – a shadow: aid workers were still (somewhat irritatingly) warning of humanitarian disasters that would occur with the setting in of winter. It rankled too that the terrorism of the tyrannical Taliban regime from which the Afghan people were being 'liberated' wasn't exactly 'international terrorism' – indeed it was definitely not 'international terrorism', more 'state terrorism' (which in the West people were reluctant to be reminded of), an internal affair. And it had never been the declared intention of the 'war against inter-national terrorism' to target 'internal state terrorism': that was a whole different game. The Taliban had been there for a considerable time and the United States hadn't bothered; the United States had never been above sponsoring a bit of state terrorism herself. It was a disquieting thought that retaliation in this case had deliberately taken place against something that wasn't its target. 'The war against international terrorism' might have claimed a petty victory if the military action had at least flushed out quickly that symbol of 'international terror' Osama bin Laden – 'dead or alive', as President Bush had said – but even this minuscule satisfaction was denied by the length and reality and scale of the military action. The final concentration on the Tora Bora mountains, whose pounding by bombs was too much like the throwing of a seismic tantrum, only added to the sense of banal absurdity of the whole situation.

So the ostensible target of the 'war against international terrorism' kept slipping through the grasp of the military action as well as that of the war of abstractions and moving elsewhere, and the longer the 'war against international terrorism' carried on the more apparent it became that in some sense it hasn't moved beyond the first step – beyond the announcement and commencement of war that took place with the 11 September bombing of the World Trade Center. Since that announcement and commencement of war there had been a long pause, in which the terror of that moment had been multiplied and transmitted rapidly to other corners of the world by an instrumentalised superpower and allies. In the meanwhile, the United States military bombed Afghanistan to bits, and aided the Northern Alliance to overthrow a deeply and rightly unpopular Taliban regime; and the United States extended the threat of similar action against other more or less similar states (none as extreme or ideologically uncompromising as the Taliban) and the people living under their jurisdiction – thus transmitting the terror and anxiety of ordinary people effectively around the world. Another way of looking at that might be to wonder whether the 'war against international terrorism' is not to some significant extent a war within the United States and her Western European allies, a war that is fought in the imagination and has terrible effects both inside and outside. The 'war against international terrorism' thus far had nothing to do with this endlessly deferred enemy: it had more to do with the visions and imaginings and Manichean impositions – all breaking down with childish simplicity into us and them, right and wrong, good and evil, white and black, West and East, democracy and Islam, etc. – that were cultivated by all those (attackers and attacked) who were involved in this war.

It may also be that this extension of terror is something that the instrumentalised state terrorism of the United States and her primarily Western allies might ease themselves out of, by using it to their own material and political ends. That could be one way of de-instrumentalising their state terroristic mechanisms, and arguably at the end of that lies a new era and a new form of imperialism.

On Saturday night, 1 December 2001, two suicide bombers blew themselves up in central Jerusalem. On Sunday 2 December, a Jewish settler was shot dead in Gaza, and a bus-bombing killed 15 people in the city of Haifa. Altogether 26 Israelis died over the weekend through terrorist attacks. On 3 December the Israeli government retaliated by bombing the official residence of Palestinian Authority's chief, Yasser Arafat, and a building of Arafat's police forces in the West Bank town of Jenin. In a speech made following the first spate of bombings, Ariel Sharon said:

> *The Palestinian Authority and Arafat, and the Palestinian Authority is Arafat, they are directly responsible for the terrible situation. It is impossible for the terrorists to carry out their actions without shelter, a hiding place. They [the PA] allowed them to train in the area, to keep their headquarters. Some of their headquarters are close to Arafat's headquarters. This plan is open to them, therefore we say Arafat is today responsible for what has happened.*
>
> *Just as the United States acts in its battle against world terror, under the brave leadership of President Bush, just as it acts with all its strength, so shall we do ... with all the means at our disposal.[11]*

More bombings occurred on 4 December in the West Bank and Gaza, in which two people died and more than 80 were wounded, mostly children, it was reported. Tacit support for these bombings was expressed by the United States through a statement made by Ari Fleischer, President Bush's spokesman, and despite some international pressure the United States refused to urge restraint on Israel. In addition to Hamas and the Islamic Jihad, who already figured in Israel's list of terrorist organisations, two further names were added: Force 17 (the personal security force of Arafat) and the Tamzin (a quasi-military force set up by Arafat as a counterweight to militant Islamic groups). The media speculated widely that Sharon was trying to target Arafat himself. The United States closed down a major Islamic charity and froze the assets of two Palestinian organisations on suspicion of funding Hamas. On 5 December Arafat yielded to the pressure

*to respond to the weekend terrorist attacks and thus stop Israeli bombings
by putting the Hamas founder, Sheikh Ahmed Yassin, under house arrest.
The bombings did stop, but the peace was all too short-lived, and both
terrorist attacks and bombings resumed in a matter of days.*

This was a tense period. The United States's special relationship
with Israel and the manner in which both states have supported each
other's state terrorist activities over an extended period have been
so extensively documented and examined that they hardly need
further comment. This reassertion of the special relationship was an
important announcement of positions. It had been observed all
through the 'war against international terrorism' as it was being
conducted until then that, in their bid to maintain the support of
the Middle Eastern states for the military action in Afghanistan, the
United States and her Western allies had been reluctant to speak in
favour of Israel and were more willing to acknowledge the wrongs
that the Palestinians had suffered. It was a matter of diplomatic sensitivity. Despite brutal acts of terrorism perpetrated by Palestinian
groups, many, even in the West, are sympathetic towards the Palestinians. The desperation underlying those acts seems
understandable, given the equal brutality of the state terrorism that
Israel directs against the Palestinian people. The Israeli action of 4
and 5 December, with United States's support, was a turning away
from that diplomatic strategy and a reassertion of the traditional
relationship.

Ariel Sharon's statement says it all. By this time the military action
in Afghanistan had almost reached the only culmination it could
conceivably have reached as a demonstration of strength and
purpose after the 11 September attacks under the pretext of being a
'war against international terrorism', the ousting of the Taliban –
and had been accepted as a legitimate response by other Middle
Eastern states, as well as by vaguely liberal sceptics within the West
and elsewhere. A precedent had been set in Middle Eastern affairs.
With that precedent, the niceties of diplomatic sensitivity didn't
need to be maintained any longer, and nor was it necessary to worry
too much about the sensitivities of all those vaguely liberal sceptics.
Ariel Sharon's statement was an assertion of that precedent and a
declaration of his determination to use that precedent in his own
context. The whole episode showed quickly, deliberately, revealingly
that under the banner of the 'war against international terrorism'
every act of political violence would become an opportunity to
further disperse the United States's instrumentalised state terrorism

through those 'friendly' states that were already her instruments. The terrorist logic that initiated the attacks of 11 September, arguably with the full expectation of the United States's response, would disperse outwards through the United States to her strategic satellites and instruments (none more staunch than Israel). The terrorist logic of the 11 September attacks merged seamlessly into the mechanical state terrorist logic of the United States's foreign policy which was absorbing within itself those that have been instrumentalised by the United States's state terrorist logic ... and outwards. Terror and counterterror and countercounterterror and so on had conjoined into a singular political process leading in an as yet indeterminate, but not unenvisagable, direction.

A frenzy of increasing the powers of security organisations and passing new antiterrorist legislation followed 11 September 2001 across the West. In the United States a large number of suspects was detained, without access to legal representation, in the process of investigating the attacks. A series of measures designed to strengthen the hand of security and policing organisations was speedily ratified – leading up to the extraordinary plans to set up military tribunals for non-United States citizens suspected of any terrorist links. The military tribunals in question, it was proposed, would each consist of a three person military court, which could meet inside or outside the country, and convict the suspect by a majority verdict. Only mild qualms were expressed, notably by the Democratic civil liberties campaigner, Senator Russell Feingold; these qualms were ackowledged 'in principle'. Presenting this proposal at a Judiciary Committee on 8 December, Attorney-General John Ashcroft stated:

> *We need honest, reasoned debate, and not fear-mongering. To those ... who scare peace-loving people with phantoms of lost liberty, my message is this: Your tactics only aid terrorists, for they erode our national unity and diminish our resolve. They give ammunition to America's enemies and pause to America's friends. They encourage people of goodwill to remain silent in the face of evil.[12]*

Reluctant to be seen encouraging terrorists, the members of the Judiciary Committee refrained from asking any difficult questions. In the United Kingdom, Home Secretary David Blunkett's Anti-Terrorism Bill caused rather more controversy, and met stiff opposition from the House of Lords – but the Bill was ultimately passed with a few modifications. On 12

December 2001 it was reported that the German government had used new anti-terrorism laws to ban at least 20 Islamic groups. The European Union sanctioned a common arrest warrant for its 15 member states for 32 crimes deemed pertinent to anti-terrorist efforts (this was held up only briefly because of a veto from the Italian premier Berlusconi, who was worried about his own nefarious interests). It is also worth mentioning a couple of related matters here. On 6 December it was reported that a 20-year-old white American Taliban fighter, John Walker, had been found. This caused some consternation in the United States, where considerable dismay and some anger was expressed. In the Western media coverage of this that followed there was speculation about whether he had been taken in and brainwashed by some cult, and about his legal position. It was felt that he could be charged with treason (which would carry a death sentence) but it also appeared that complicated legal technicalities made this difficult. On a different note, reports had appeared as early as 11 November of an amateur video which recorded a conversation involving Osama bin Laden, wherein he admitted masterminding the 11 September attacks. This was to be publicly released as evidence against bin Laden, but that was held up till 13 December by the practicalities of presenting it. Amongst other things, it needed to be subtitled or dubbed in English, and examined for authenticity. It was reported that bin Laden was clearly aware that he was being recorded.

Since the 11 September attacks on the World Trade Center the people of the United States and Western Europe had been waiting to register an *engagement* in the 'war against international terrorism' that would give it a quality of being a war, with force being used – or at least being shown to exist – and with some sense of initial equivalence from the two opposed parties. This meant that, since the declaration and commencement of war on 11 September, and throughout the following months of negotiation of abstractions and military action, a sign had been awaited from the opposition – the 'international terrorists' – that would confirm that the ongoing war was a war, and a just (if not infinitely just) war. Such a sign of engagement could only be another act of terrorism, large or small in scale, that could be clearly attributed to 'international terrorists', hopefully from al-Quaeda or some other Islamic group. This might sound perverse: can I really be suggesting that the people of the United States and Western Europe were actually looking forward to and hoping for another 'international terrorist' attack amongst them? Of course not looking forward to it, but certainly expecting it

– without any pleasurable sensation (what an idea), but with fear and anxiety. But, I also feel, the people were paradoxically hoping it would happen and be done with, be finished, so that the tension would be over and all would be clear (that there is a war afoot and that whatever then needs to be done must be done). Defence and security forces were warning of new terrorist attacks regularly, the antiterrorist legislation was deemed to be appropriate given the dangers. The anthrax attacks promised to be almost a confirmation of that expectation, and it is not insignificant that interest in them waned once it became clear that no external – 'international terrorist' – source could be linked to them, that these attacks were more likely to have had a domestic origin within the United States. Does a domestic origin mean that the international terrorism of the anthrax attacks was any the less scary? In practice clearly not, but in effect it turned out under those circumstances to be less scary than the same anthrax attacks clearly linked, say, to al-Quaeda. The inference seems reasonably clear: even while the people of the United States and Western Europe were in the throes of anxiety and fear about possible 'international terrorist' attacks, they were also in some sense waiting from them to happen – to confirm that a war was afoot – to clarify the situation.

As it happened, despite repeated warnings the string of expected terrorist attacks which would have indicated an ongoing engagement of 'international terrorists', or to be precise of Islamic 'international terrorists', in a war against the West did not materialise in the few months following 11 September. But meanwhile the frenzy of antiterrorist legislation had only increased and intensified – antiterrorist legislation which could, however benignly read, be used in principle not just to curtail civil liberties but also to violate human rights, particularly of immigrant groups and dissident political formations within the United States and Western European countries. Such acts of group terrorism (as opposed to state terrorism) as did occur in this period occurred where they normally do: in Israel, in India, in Sri Lanka. The antiterrorist legislation, which was proceeding with the assumption of a war situation – the abnormality of a war situation has conventionally been adequate grounds for the suspension of normal civil liberties and human rights – was beginning to acquire a life of its own: it could be suspected that the legislation was as much *creating and perpetuating* the war situation as responding to it.

Ashcroft's statement (quoted above) shows a deeply cynical grasp of the whole situation. Is it possible that he doesn't see the irony of championing an 'honest, reasoned debate' while recommending that a whole intensively contemplated, highly valued and carefully constructed perspective – that of 'civil liberties' – be banned and censored? However much faith one may have in the probity and judgement of the United States government and military (not unremarkably, many don't have much), it is undeniable that a principle is established in the idea of military tribunals for suspects who are not United States citizens (not to speak of the scope for injustices inherent in their structure) that in the eyes of the law in the United States (which would also operate outside the United States) there is going to be differential treatment of different peoples on the grounds of their nationality and only on the grounds of their nationality. In principle, distinctions could be made between two people, who might have committed exactly the same crimes for the same reasons with the same effects, on the grounds of their different nationalities. A terrorist from the far right, who is a citizen of the United States and blows up, say, a building full of innocent people in Oklahoma because of his beliefs, would be treated differently from a terrorist from some Islamic group, who is a citizen of Saudi Arabia, who does the same thing. The former would be treated as a civilian (facing a civilian court), the latter as a combatant (facing a military tribunal). The structure of the civilian court is such that what would be regarded as a fair trial is always likely; the structure of the military tribunal is designedly such that the trial could almost never be regarded as fair. Even in a war situation, it has conventionally been recommended that for legal purposes a strict distinction between civilian and combatant be maintained (though it is seldom adhered to in practice). In principle then, anyone who is not a United States citizen could be regarded by the military tribunals as a combatant. And in principle also, in certain areas United States law could begin to be regarded as international law that is designed to discriminate in favour of United States citizens.

It seems to me to be impossible that these implications of that particular plan could not have been clear to the people of the United States and their representatives. It needed a great deal of conscious *unthinkingness*, or a genuinely undemocratic and discriminatory bent of mind, to be able to overlook them.

Some of the disquiet that was expressed in the media about John Walker, the white American Taliban fighter, derived no doubt from the discriminatory implications of the legislative practices that were already beginning to materialise in the course of the 'war on international terrorism' in early December 2001. He became a kind of test case: either he was that United States citizen who could get away with it in a manner in which no other Taliban fighter who wasn't, whether Afghan or not, could hope to; or he was just another Taliban fighter (possibly worse, since he could be regarded as a traitor to his own country) who would be treated at least as severely as any other combatant and suspected 'international terrorist' would be. In the event, in his particular case the media were as inclined to be charitable as they were to be outraged. Was he brainwashed by a cult? It was asked with an air of wondering whether that might not provide mitigating circumstances. But by that argument the entire Taliban and al-Quaeda formations could be regarded as cults and most Taliban fighters and other 'international terrorists' (including the immediate perpetrators of the 11 September attacks) could be regarded as brainwashed victims. Few wondered whether he didn't have 'international terrorist' connections and culpabilities; there is no doubt that had he not been a United States citizen *and* white this would have been mooted without compunction. The emerging consensus seems to be that he should be regarded as some sort of quirk, an eccentricity, an aberration, who shouldn't be taken seriously – even by the law. But that is unlikely to fool anyone: he was regarded as someone who deserves some sort of special dispensation because it was *unthinkingly* inconceivable that any white United States citizen could be an Islamic 'international terrorist' and Taliban warrior. But that is nonsense – why can United States citizens (white, black or brown) not be 'international terrorists' of some persuasion? And does it make any difference whether 'international terrorism' occurs in the name of Islamic convictions or, for instance, of white supremacist or Christian convictions?

There emerges through these ruminations mediated through the United States media and the post-11-September antiterrorist legislation the vague form of an idea – gradually growing distinct. It is ultimately a religious idea which contradicts all notions of globalisation and liberal democracy and civil liberties that the United States and Western European states have particularly and ostentatiously championed at least in principle (if not in practice, and even if these ideas can themselves appear unsatisfactory in various ways): the idea of being *chosen people*, which usually gets echoed crudely and blatantly in ultranationalist discourses, and which can always get perverted into some model of biogenetic supremacy.

Legal questions and media mediations also surround the issue of the video of bin Laden's admission of masterminding the 11 September attacks in the United States. It seems to bring the perpetrators and bin Laden/al-Quaeda (whom I kept distinct in Chapter 4 above) together at last. The video was released after long notice, accompanied by some unusually emotive reportage in newspapers and television news broadcasts. It was felt that the whole military action against Taliban-ruled Afghanistan had at last, and in retrospect, been justified. The kind of distinction I made in Chapter 4 between the perpetrators and bin Laden/al-Quaeda would now no longer have to be maintained. It was extraordinarily fortuitous that the discovery of this video was made, and it is not unworthy of speculation whether bin Laden (who was, it appears, aware of the video being made) wished it to be discovered. From a legal point of view this is clearly admissible evidence and, by the sounds of it, clinching evidence, though it would be interesting to find out what a defence lawyer might make of it in a United States court of law. Would a recorded confession be enough evidence to convict? What sort of supporting circumstantial evidence goes with it apart from the early suspicion and conviction that bin Laden/al-Quaeda were responsible? But these are matters of legalistic debate which do not affect the fact that at least those within the United States and Western Europe, and others who have supported the military action with some inclination to believe in bin Laden's guilt and yet some vestiges of doubt at the back of their minds, would now be convinced. In Chapter 4 I mentioned the importance of creating at least an environment in which there can be unambiguous conviction about the guilt of the accused. Within the context of the military action of the United States and her allies, this video might well be instrumental in creating that environment. Its most significant aspect is that it presents evidence to the people who are represented by the governments who undertook that military action.

But that, regrettably, won't erase the fact that the distinction between bin Laden/al-Quaeda and the perpetrators that I made in Chapter 4 remains valid. The video came after the assumption of guilt had been made and the whole expensive military action was under way. If this is, as some newspapers said, 'the most damning evidence yet' against bin Laden, it is clear that when the military action was planned and undertaken with the intention of getting bin Laden 'dead or alive', the evidence must have been purely circumstantial and most likely speculative and weak. From the perspective of legal principle (I won't argue this at length) the assumption of guilt as being enough to initiate proceedings of the kind that were undertaken is more worrying than the proof of guilt in retrospect. In the process of the 'war against international terrorism' both as military action and in abstractions that followed the events of 11 September, the distinction between bin Laden/al-Quaeda and the perpetrators was not only valid but had full play. The video might seem in retrospect to justify entirely that 'war against international terrorism'; but the process through which that war unfolded and was conducted tells us more significantly what future 'wars against international terrorism' might look like. 'Wars against international terrorism' can be of a massive scale without having much regard for legal process, may gradually lose the legal objective altogether, may acquire an end and a series of connotations that have little to do with the act of 'international terrorism' that they ostensibly redress, may be an instrumentalised continuation of terror itself.

But then the proof of bin Laden's guilt and the fall of the Taliban – and for that matter, the capture and execution or death of bin Laden (yet to occur) – wouldn't be the end of this 'war against international terrorism'.

When the United States formed the international coalition against terror and initiated the 'war against international terrorism' soon after 11 September 2001, she made it clear that the military action against Afghanistan would be simply a first step – the final objective would be the reasonable suppression of 'international terrorism' itself, the quelling of 'international terrorists' at large and of those who 'harbour them'. There was only one ruling Taliban and one bin Laden, and their erasure wouldn't meet these objectives. Al-Quaeda however, as United States intelligence asserts and the media report, and by the middle of December 2001 numerous books testify, is an international network, with cells in a large number of countries, and can be linked to pretty well any Islamic political or charitable or financial organisation. It is a moot issue whether the countries which these alleged al-Quaeda cells with their protean manifestations appear in are aware of their existence – can some or most or all of them be regarded as harbourers? The number of 'rogue states' in the United States' list has multiplied significantly, and with it the licence to bomb or otherwise attack these countries. When the anthrax attacks occurred in September and October there was speculation in the media – not without some guidance from United States intelligence sources – that links with Iraq could not be ruled out. Iraq was however too diplomatically sensitive an issue at the time to be meddled with. On 22 November the United States had forced the closure of two companies in Somalia – the only internet company, Somalia Internet Co., and the only telecommunications business, al-Barakaat, in the country. This was reported at the time with mild concern, since it appeared that about 80 per cent of the Somalian population was dependent on money transfer operations from friends and family abroad, and such closures could have devastating economic consequences. Somalia is one of the poorest countries of the world. On 10 December it was reported that a terror hit list of places that were less diplomatically sensitive than Iraq had been drawn up by the United States military, including the Aceh region in Indonesia, the Hadhramaut valley in Yemen, and the Ras Khomboni region in Southern Somalia. Somalia's interim Prime Minister Hassan Abshir Farah (of the Transitional National Government), whose control over Somalian territory was limited, rejected charges of hosting organisations with al-Quaeda connections, and invited the Bush administration to inspect their military bases. The invitation was refused. On 11 December it appeared that United States military personnel had already visited the city Baiboa in Somalia (controlled by the Rahanwein Resistance Army, an organisation that opposes the Transitional National Government with Ethiopian support) and had met with opposition warlords, focusing on the activities of an Islamic group, al-Itihaad al-Islamiya. A beefed-up United States naval presence along the Somali coast and around the Gulf of Aden was observed. The United States government expressed a determination to root out all al-Quaeda terrorists in Somalia, maintaining at the same time that this would not require large scale bombing as in Afghanistan and could be accomplished by small raids.

The 'war against international terrorism' would, the Bush administration had promised, be one that would last a long time and be fought on many fronts.

This study was written in the context of developments after 11 September 2001 from sources (mainly media reports) available within and presenting perspectives that seemed relevant within the United States, Britain and some other Western European countries. It is not intended to examine what precisely the causes behind the 11 September terrorist attacks in the United States, and what the political-philosophical nuances of those causes are; it is intended as an examination of the aftermath of the 11 September attacks, and as a clarification of some of the political-philosophical nuances of that aftermath from the specific context in which it was written. As such therefore, it is an attempt to gain a political-philosophical perspective on a happening political sphere while it was happening – without any preconceptions about the need for analytical distance, but with a determination to avoid the kind of *unthinkingness* that I have mentioned above, and with some understanding of the existing political-philosophical thinking that might be relevant to the events in question. It seems to me that this attempt may well be one way of resisting the barrage of *unthinkingness* which I felt bombarded by as well as the overwhelming effect of images and attitudes transmitted (often with insidious effect) by the media. As regards the causes of the terrorist attacks of 11 September in the United States, and their roots within the Middle East and in relations between the Middle East and the West, valuable studies appeared soon after that tragedy which are worth mentioning. Especially strong on an apprehension of the situation within the Middle East, and the history of relations between the Middle East and the West, insofar as these have a bearing on the terrorist attacks of 11 September (areas that this study has not concerned itself with at all) are some of the essays in *How Did This Happen: Terrorism and the New War*,[13] and especially Fred Halliday's *Two Hours that Shook the World*.[14]

Fred Halliday's several earlier studies of Islamic culture and the history of the Middle East are also illuminating in retrospect apropos 11 September, and indeed in placing the 'war against international terrorism' in a historical perspective.[15] In *Two Hours*, Halliday issues cautionary statements for those who respond to events such as the ones of 11 September, enjoining what I read as an appeal for *thinkingness*. Thus Halliday rightly warns against simplistic generalisations and oppositions, denounces the use of unthinking rhetoric about the clash of cultures or civilisations, tries to give a sense of the complexities that are hidden behind terms like the West or the Arab world or the United States, and analyses such widespread phenomena as 'anti-Muslimism' and 'Islamophobia' in Europe and the United States, as well as 'hostility to the USA' from conservative and left-wing factions in Europe and within the United States, and the 'anti-Americanism' of the Middle East. These are very much worth keeping in mind. In his zeal for thoughtful balance Halliday makes several interesting comments about the anti-United States arguments of the left and the reality of the United States as he sees it. After mentioning some of the well-known low points of United States foreign policy and culture ('Vietnam, Nicaragua, the neglect of

Palestinian rights, Cuba, the grotesque irresponsibility of its gun laws and its media, the insidious role of religion and money in the public life')[16] he goes on to say:

> Much is made, especially in recent days, of American militarism and belligerency: this is, the discourse of cowboys culture aside, a myth. No other major country has a record as cautious and restrained as the USA: it had to be dragged into World War in 1941, at it was dragged into Bosnia in 1995. The USA fought these wars in the 1990s – Kuwait in 1991, Bosnia 1995, Kosovo 1999 – all in response to aggression against Muslim people. Sneering at American aggressiveness comes strangely from other countries given their record in modern times: Britain and France, who trampled over half of Asia and Africa, Russia and China, not to mention Germany, Italy and Japan.
>
> This denunciation of America is detached from any concrete, informed assessment of US policy in the period since the cold war. Under the Clinton administration, the US record was far from perfect but in a range of issues, from international economic and human rights conflicts through to specific areas of conflict, it did engage in a constructive manner. Moreover the idea that all the ills of the world can be blamed on the USA, or on its state and citizens, is simplistic indeed.[17]

This was written shortly after the 11 September attacks. But Halliday had clearly had similar feelings before: one of the essays published in *Two Hours* is 'The Other Stereotype: America and Its Critics', dated 1991, in which left-wing critics of the United States particularly are castigated for their opposition to 'intervention as such, in all its forms'[18] – and it is argued that though United States intervention has been understandably self-interested it has also been positive (the United States has effectively liberated people from tyrannical regimes and at the behest of those people). Left-wing critics are also accused of the following:

> Faced with the monolithic consensus of the mainstream media and academic output, the opposition has too often tended to resort to conspiracy theory, scandal and moral denunciation. Conspiracy and scandal there certainly are, but in themselves they do not constitute an adequate alternative analysis. What has too often happened is that these facile critiques from the European and US

Lefts have fed into the conspiracy theories generated in the third world itself: instead of providing analysis that is informed, and which enables action, it often misleads and disables.[19]

I have quoted the above at some length because I feel that the tenor of these cautions are worth noting for the left-wing critics in question. But I also quote them because they present some interesting demonstrations of *unthinkingness* that need to be pondered. *Unthinkingness* appears in unexpected places. There is clearly a change of tone from 1991 to 2001 regarding Halliday's view of the United States: in the early nineties the appearance of United States's state terrorism was still so blatant that it always had to be taken into account; by the beginning of the new millennium a quick and forgetful listing of Vietnam, Nicaragua, Cuba (only?) mixed up with gun laws and media enables Halliday soon afterwards to declare the United States's caution and restraint in military matters in one wide sweep from the Second World War in 1941 to Bosnia in 1995. For Halliday, in 1991 the United States's interventionism seemed 'self-interested' but nevertheless salutary; in 2001 the United States's interventionism has become altruistic so that intervention in Kuwait, Bosnia, Kosovo were all merely a 'response to aggression against Muslim people' (is that how Iraq's invasion of Kuwait should be read? is that all that the United States was concerned about?). In 1991 the United States was a bit militaristic (but generally in a manner to be applauded), in 2001 the United States's militarism is a myth (she has to be dragged, against her will, into wars). But these little shifts and misrepresentations in the interests of making a worthy point are a small matter: more interesting (unthinking?) shifts are discernable in Halliday's warning to ill-informed and ungrateful left-wing critics. If I read the above statements correctly these smack of a certain overdetermination of regional location in the enunciation of ideological positions. So, it seems that no critic (conservative or left) in Britain or France should criticise the United States's imperialistic militarism because Britain and France have had a record of world-wide imperialism themselves. This argument is very difficult to understand. If Halliday means that it is inconsistent to be proud of British militarism and critical of the United States's militarism then, of course, it makes sense. If he means that all left and conservative thinkers within Britain should not dare to be critical of the United States's ongoing imperialism out of some sort of regard for Britain's history then, of course, it is nonsense. The problem is that Halliday's statement could so easily be read in the latter fashion. In a similar mould, another argument that baffles is the warning that the left of the United States and Europe should be careful not to feed into 'conspiracy theories' of the Third World. Though Halliday uses 'conspiracy theories' with all the inflexions of incredulity that that phrase attracts, he does say that conspiracies do occur. There is just a hint of the patronising about his view of the Third World (this generalisation hadn't been dissected): but let's overlook that. Is the crucial question: What is the truth about these conspiracy theories and how does the truth affect peoples of different parts of the world? Or is it: Who is allowed to have conspiracy theories and who isn't? Halliday's statement seems to give priority to the second question. I am convinced priority should be given to the first. I feel it is important to try to get at some sort of truth in relation to the theories that concern me, and to declare to *all* (irrespective of where I am and where my audience may be) the reasons why I have reached the conclusions that I have. Only then can I engage with those who disagree.

Oxford, 15 December 2001

Notes

CHAPTER 1

1. Martin Shaw, *Civil Society and Media in Global Crises: Representing Distant Violence* (London: Pinter, 1996), p.8.
2. Conor Gearty, *The Future of Terrorism* (London: Phoenix, 1997), p.14.
3. Todd Sandler and Walter Enders, 'Is Transnational Terrorism Becoming More Threatening?', *Journal of Conflict Resolution* 44:3, 2000, p.329.
4. Noam Chomsky and Edward S. Herman, *Manufacturing Consent: The Political Economy of the Mass Media* (New York: Pantheon, 1988); Noam Chomsky, *Necessary Illusions: Thought Control and Democratic Society* (London: Pluto Press, 1989); Edward S. Herman, *The Real Terror Network: Terrorism in Fact and Propaganda* (Boston: South End, 1982); Michael Parenti, *Inventing Reality: The Politics of the News Media* (New York: St. Martin's Press, 1992); John Pilger, *Hidden Agendas* (London: Vintage, 1998); David McGowan, *Derailing Democracy: The America the Media Don't Want You to See* (Monroe, Maine: Common Courage, 2000) .
5. Noam Chomsky, *World Orders, Old and New* (London: Pluto Press, 1994), p.69.

CHAPTER 2

1. Toby Helm, 'Terror Strike a "Work of Art"', *Daily Telegraph* at telegraph.co.uk, 19 September 2001.
2. Jean Baudrillard, *The Consumer Society: Myths and Strictures* (London: Sage, 1970/1998), p.34.
3. See, for example, Walter Laqueur, 'The Futility of Terrorism', *Harper's* 252:1510, March 1976, p.104; Walter Laqueur, *Terrorism* (London: Weidenfeld & Nicolson, 1977), pp.109–110; Yonah Alexander, 'Terrorism and the Media: Some Considerations', in Yonah Alexander, David Carlton and Paul Wilkinson (eds), *Terrorism: Theory and Practice* (Boulder, Colo.: Westview, 1979), pp.159–174; Yonah Alexander, 'Terrorism and the Media in the Middle East', in Yonah Alexander and S.M. Finger (eds), *Terrorism: Interdisciplinary Perspectives* (New York: John Jay, 1977), pp.166–206.
4. Amy Sands Redlick, 'The Transnational Flow of Information as a Cause of Terrorism', in Alexander, Carlton and Wilkinson (eds) (1979), p.91.
5. Alex P. Schmid and Janny de Graaf, *Violence as Communication: Insurgent Terrorism and the Western News Media* (London: Sage, 1982), p.1.
6. See, for example, Brigette L. Nacos, 'Accomplice or Witness: The Media's Role in Terrorism', *Current History* 99:636, April 2000, pp.174–179.
7. Some of the arguments surrounding censorship of media coverage of terrorist statements (drawing on the experience of legal appeals against the banning of IRA interviews in Britain) are usefully given in Paul

Gilbert, 'The Oxygen of Publicity: Terrorism and Reporting Restriction', in Andrew Belsey and Ruth Chadwick (eds), *Ethical Issues in Journalism and the Media* (London: Routledge, 1992), pp.137–153; an early exhortation, often repeated thereafter, for the press simply to be responsible and self-aware is found in H.H.A. Cooper, 'Terrorism and the Media', in Alexander and Finger (eds) (1977), pp.141–156; the setting up of regulatory bodies is recommended in Richard Clutterbuck, *The Media and Political Violence* (London: Macmillan, 1981), pp.161–162. That the media need to be curbed somehow apropos reportage on terrorism is the theme of almost all the essays on the role of the media in Benjamin Netanyahu (ed.), *Terrorism: How the West can Win* (New York: Farrar Straus Giroux, 1986).

8. Edward S. Herman, *The Real Terror Network* (Boston: South End, 1982). See Chapter 1, note 4 for 'the others'.

9. Philip Schlesinger, Graham Murdock and Philip Elliott, *Televising Terrorism: Political Violence in Popular Culture* (London: Comedia, 1983), especially Chapters 5 and 6.

10. Carol W. Lewis, 'The Terror That Failed: Public Opinion in the Aftermath of the Bombing in Oklahoma City', *Public Administration Review* 60:3, May 2000, pp.201–210.

11. Michelle Slone, 'Responses to Media Coverage of Terrorism', *Journal of Conflict Resolution* 44:4, 2000, pp.508–522.

12. N. Gowing, 'Real-Time Television Coverage of Armed Conflicts and Diplomatic Crises: Does it Pressure or Distort Foreign Policy Decisions?', Working Paper 94–97, Shorenstein Barone Center on the Press, Politics and Public Policy, Harvard University, 1994.

13. Martin Shaw, *Civil Society and Media in Global Crises* (London: Pinter, 1996); I. Volkmer, *News in the Global Media* (Luton: University of Luton Press, 1999).

14. It is worth noting though in this context that Richard Boyd, 'Representing Political Violence: The Mainstream Media and the Weatherman "Days of Rage"', *American Studies* 41:1, Spring 2000, pp.141–164, has argued that the media make and uphold the distinction between legitimate and illegitimate violence.

15. '[...] the violence employed in terrorism is aimed partly at destabilizing the existing political or social order but mainly at publicizing the goals or the cause espoused by the terrorists. Hence the eagerness of terrorists to take credit for their acts of violence; indeed, whenever an act of violence is not "claimed" by some terrorist organization this is presumptive evidence that the act in question is not committed by terrorists', says Burleigh Taylor Wilkins in *Terrorism and Collective Responsibility* (London: Routledge, 1992), p.3. Stephen R. Bowers and Kimberley R. Keys also note, however, the emergence of a trend of 'silent terrorism' (terrorist attacks for which responsibility hasn't been claimed) since the mid nineteen-eighties, and they discuss a few such incidents in 'Technology and Terrorism: The New Threat for the Millennium', *Conflict Studies* 309, May 1998, p.3.

16. '[...] it is not the magnitude of the terrorist operation that counts but the publicity', observed Walter Laqueur in *Terrorism*, p.109.

17. See Schlesinger, Murdoch and Elliot, *Televising Terrorism*, pp.156–159.
18. Schmid and de Graaf, *Violence as Communication*, p.15.
19. *Guardian*, 28 September 2001, p.5.

CHAPTER 3

1. It would be rather pointless to list the numerous and generally familiar works of these prominent revolutionary thinkers that discuss the rationale and conduct of political violence for the realisation of a revolutionary state. The manner in which these works have been appropriated into discussions on what has since the nineteen-sixties been called 'insurgent terrorism' and 'social terror' (with the pejorative sense that is implied by these terms) can be gauged from papers such as the following: Joan Witte, 'Violence in Lenin's Thought and Practice: The Spark and the Conflagration', *Terrorism and Political Violence* 5:3, Autumn 1993, pp.135–203; Raphael Cohen-Almager, 'Foundations of Violence, Terror and War in the Writings of Marx, Engels and Lenin', *Terrorism and Political Violence* 3:2, Summer 1991, pp.1–24; John W. Williams, 'Carlos Marighella: The Father of Urban Guerrilla Warfare', *Terrorism – An International Journal* 12:1, 1989, pp.1–20; Hanno Hardt, Luis Rivera-Perec and Jorge A. Callas-Santillana, 'The Death and Resurrection of Ernesto Che Guevara: US Media and the Deconstruction of a Revolutionary Life', *International Journal of Cultural Studies* 1:3, 1998, pp.351–372; Tu Wei-ming, 'Destructive Will and Ideological Holocaust: Maoism as a Source of Social Suffering in China', *Daedalus* 125:1, Winter 1996, pp.149–180.

2. The manner in which violence is always implicit in a colonial situation and explodes into a decolonisation movement is most influentially theorised by Frantz Fanon, *The Wretched of the Earth*, trans. Constance Karrington (Harmondsworth: Penguin, 1961/1963), and Aimé Césaire, *Discourse on Colonialism*, trans. Joan Pinkham (New York: Monthly Review Press, 1955/1972).

3. Those who tend to see Sartre as a prophet of political terror often draw on the most diverse and unexpected selection of his writings – again, I feel it is pointless to make a list of these. The arguments which are adduced to bring Sartre into the fold of 'terrorist theory' (usually with stronger ideological motivation than academic integrity) can be gauged from such articles as Matthew Mackenzie, 'Jean-Paul Sartre on Violence and Terror', *Terrorism and Political Violence* 6:4, Winter 1994, pp.476–506. Georges Sorel's contribution to the consideration of political violence is confined to a single book – Georges Sorel, *Reflections on Violence*, trans. T.E. Hulme and J. Roth (New York: Collier, 1950). For a useful discussion of this under the banner of terrorism, see Malcolm Anderson, 'Georges Sorel: Reflections on Violence', *Terrorism and Political Violence* 1:1, January 1989, pp.70–78.

4. Since I wrote this book my attention has been drawn to the work of Donald J. Hanle, *Terrorism: The Newest Face of Warfare* (New York: Pergamon, 1989), which has a detailed discussion of the theoretical and practical arguments that may attach to discerning whether terrorism

may be considered to be warfare. Some of this agrees with what I have to say here, and it is a far more searching consideration of the matter than I have undertaken – but since I developed these arguments without its aid I let them stand without any mention of Hanle's book beyond this note.

5. Edward Hyams, *Terrorists and Terrorism* (London: J.M. Dent, 1975), pp.9–13.

6. Burleigh Taylor Wilkins, *Terrorism and Collective Responsibility* (London: Routledge, 1992). The three specific consequentialist arguments that he addresses are found in: R.M. Hare, 'On Terrorism', *Journal of Value Inquiry* 13, Winter 1979; Kai Nielsen, 'On Terrorism and Political Assassination', in Harold M. Zellner (ed.), *Assassination* (Cambridge, Mass., 1974); and Ted Honderich, 'Four Conclusions About Violence of the Left', *Canadian Journal of Philosophy* 9, June 1979.

7. Carl von Clausewitz, *On War*, ed. and trans. Michael Howard and Peter Paret (Princeton: Princeton University Press, 1976), p.75.

8. The manner in which Clausewitz's notion of absolute war has been misused or misinterpreted over an extended period of military theorising is charted out in some detail in Christopher Bassford, *Clausewitz in English: The Reception of Clausewitz in Britain and America 1815–1945* (New York: Oxford University Press, 1994). The concept of absolute war, Bassford shows for the period he deals with, has often been used to dismiss Clausewitz's work as a whole. Clausewitz became more than respectable after the Second World War, according to Bassford, because:

> The prospect of nuclear war was itself a new problem, one that turned Clausewitz's concept of 'absolute war' from an abstract concept into a potential reality. The reality also perforce brought to the fore another and contrary Clausewitzian concept, that of limited war, which had seemed to most so inapplicable to warfare in the first half of the twentieth century. As for the Cold War, the widespread perception that Clausewitz's ideas underlay much of Marxist-Leninist and possibly Maoist military theory was also a major impetus to the study of *On War*. These factors sufficed to bring Clausewitz into the intellectual mainstream, but it was only the disaster in Vietnam that led American military institutions to turn to his guidance. (pp. 200–201)

In the context of Clausewitz, and in view of arguments about guerrilla warfare that are considered later in this chapter, the following article may also be of interest to the reader: Werner Hahlweg, 'Clausewitz and Guerrilla Warfare', in Michael I. Handel (ed.), *Clausewitz and Modern Strategy* (London: Frank Cass, 1986), pp.127–133.

9. Jean-Paul Sartre, *Critique of Dialectical Reason, Volume 2*, trans. Quintin Hoare (London: Verso, 1991).

10. Clausewitz, *On War*, p.77.

11. Quincy Wright, *A Study of War* (Chicago: University of Chicago Press, 1965/1992), p.8.

12. Ibid.

13. Ibid., p.9.
14. Ibid., p.698.
15. Everett L. Wheeler, 'Terrorism and Military Theory: An Historical Perspective', *Terrorism and Political Violence* 3:1, Summer 1991, p.21.
16. Walter Laqueur, *Terrorism*, p.5.
17. Ariel Merari, 'Terrorism as a Strategy of Insurgency,' *Terrorism and Political Violence* 5:4, Winter 1993, p.213.
18. Ibid., p.225.
19. Ibid., p.226.
20. Che Guevara, *Guerrilla Warfare* (Manchester: Manchester University Press, 1985), p.53.
21. Michael Walzer, *Just and Unjust Wars* (New York: Basic, 1977), p.197.
22. See, for example, David George, 'Terrorists or Freedom Fighters', in Martin Warner and Roger Crisp (eds), *Terrorism, Protest and Power* (Aldershot: Edward Elgar, 1990), pp.57–60.

CHAPTER 4

1. See Chapter 3 note 13.
2. On this see Chris Ryan, 'Tourism, Terrorism and Violence: The Risks of Wider World Travel', *Conflict Studies* 244, September 1991, pp.1–30.
3. Stansfield Turner, *Terrorism and Democracy* (Boston: Houghton Mifflin, 1991), p. 234.
4. Michele L. Malvesti, 'Explaining the United States' Decision to Strike Back at Terrorists', *Terrorism and Political Violence* 13:2, Summer 2001, p.86.
5. Concepts of a minimal state are discussed influentially and at length in Fredrick Hayek, *The Constitution of Liberty* (London: Routledge & Kegan Paul, 1960), and in Robert Nozick, *Anarchy, State and Utopia* (Oxford: Basil Blackwell, 1974).
6. Malvesti, 'Decision to Strike Back', p.99.
7. Alex P. Schmid, 'Terrorism and Democracy', *Terrorism and Political Violence* 4:4, Winter 1992, p.14.
8. Kenneth Waltz, *Theory of International Politics* (New York: McGraw-Hill, 1979). Anarchy in international politics is explained in pp.104–105, and the *realpolitik* of international politics in pp.111–117.
9. Some sense of the objections that have been raised to Waltz's formulations can be gleaned from overviews of theorisations in international relations, such as Brian C. Schmidt, *The Political Discourse of Anarchy* (Albany, N.Y.: State University of New York, 1998); Barry Buzan, Charles Jones and Richard Little, *The Logic of Anarchy* (New York: Columbia University Press, 1993); and D.S. Jarvis, *International Relations and the Challenge of Postmodernism* (Columbia, S.C.: University of South Carolina Press, 2000).
10. Ted Honderich, *Three Essays on Political Violence* (Oxford: Basil Blackwell, 1976), p.103.
11. William Bain, 'The Tyranny of Benevolence: National Security, Human Security and the Practice of Statecraft', *Global Society* 15:3, July 2001, pp.277–294.

12. Ibid., p.293.
13. Ronald D. Crelinsten, 'Terrorism, Counter-Terrorism and Democracy: The Assessment of National Security Threats', *Terrorism and Political Violence* 2:4, Winter 1990, p.244.
14. Suman Gupta, *Marxism, History and Intellectuals* (Madison, N.J.: Fairleigh Dickinson University Press, 2000) and *Corporate Capitalism and Political Philosophy* (London: Pluto Press, 2002).
15. R.M. Hare, *Moral Thinking: Its Levels, Method and Point* (Oxford: Clarendon Press, 1981), p.172.
16. Ibid., p.171.
17. Maxwell Taylor and Helen Ryan, 'Fanaticism, Political Suicide and Terror', *Terrorism – An International Journal* 12:1, 1989, pp.92–93.

CHAPTER 5

1. Interview with Noam Chomsky on Radio B92, Belgrade, after the 11 September attacks, published as 'Same Terror, New Target' in *The Times of India*, 24 September 2001. Chomsky's views on developments since 11 September are also expressed in a number of audio talks, interviews and brief comments which are most easily accessible at the time of writing on the Internet: a short piece entitled 'Response' (8 October), at http://www.zmag.org/chomreac.htm; transcription of an interview with Peter Clarke on the Australian Broadcasting Corporation programme 'Late Night Live' (16 October) entitled 'Doing the Sensible Thing', at http:/monkeyfist.com/ChomskyArchive/interviews/sensible_html; and the transcription of an audio talk at the Technology and Culture Forum at MIT (18 October), at http:/www.zmag.org/GlobalWatch/chomskymit.htm. A collection of Chomsky's interviews in the month of September 2001 was published in November 2001, *9–11* (New York: Seven Stories, 2001).
2. This includes his writings about US intervention in Vietnam especially and Asia generally in *American Power and the New Mandarins* (New York: Vintage, 1969), *At War With Asia* (London: Fontana, 1971), *Backroom Boys* (London: Fontana, 1973), *For Reasons of State* (New York: Pantheon, 1973); on US foreign policy with regard to South America in *The Culture of Terrorism* (London: Pluto Press, 1988), *On Power and Ideology* (Boston: South End, 1987), *Turning the Tide* (Boston: South End, 1985); on US manipulation of Middle Eastern affairs and especially through Israel in *The Fateful Triangle* (London: Pluto Press, 1983); on US power politics since the Cold War generally in *Terrorizing the Neighbourhood* (Stirling: AK Press, 1991), *World Orders, Old and New* (London: Pluto Press, 1994), *Acts of Aggression* (New York: Seven Stories, 1999), *The New Military Humanism* (London: Pluto Press, 1999), *The Umbrella of US Power* (New York: Seven Stories, 1999), *Profit Over People* (New York: Seven Stories, 1999), *A New Generation Draws the Line* (London: Verso, 2000); and on control of media and propaganda in the US (with Edward S. Herman) in *Manufacturing Consent* (New York: Pantheon, 1988), *Necessary Illusions* (London: Pluto Press, 1989), *Deterring Democracy* (London: Verso, 1991).

3. Some of the works that come to mind are Edward S. Herman, *The Real Terror Network* (Boston: South End, 1982); John Pilger, *Hidden Agendas* (London: Vintage, 1998); Michael McClintock, *The American Connection* (2 vols) (London: Zed, 1985); Michael McClintock, *Instruments of Statecraft* (New York: Pantheon, 1992); Lees Koonings and Dirk Krujit (eds), *Societies of Fear* (London: Zed, 1999); David McGowan, *Derailing Democracy* (Monroe, Maine: Common Courage, 2000); Alexander George (ed.), *Western State Terrorism* (Cambridge: Polity, 1991); Phyllis Bennis and Erskine Childers, *Calling the Shots* (Northampton, Mass.: Interlink, 2000); William Blum, *Killing Hope* (Monroe, Maine: Common Courage, 1995); William Blum, *Rogue State* (Monroe, Maine: Common Courage, 2000); William Blum, *The CIA* (London: Zed, 1983); Michael Parenti, *Against Empire* (San Francisco: City Lights, 1995); Michael Parenti, *Inventing Reality* (New York: St. Martin's Press, 1992); Michael Parenti, *The Sword and the Dollar* (New York: St. Martin's Press, 1989); Howard Zinn, *The Twentieth Century* (New York: Harper Perennial, 1998); Howard Zinn, *Howard Zinn on War* (New York: Seven Stories, 2000).
4. Francis Fukuyama, *The End of History and the Last Man* (Harmondsworth: Penguin, 1992).
5. Exactly along these lines is Jacques Derrida's reading of Fukuyama in *Specters of Marx*, trans. Peggy Kamuf (New York: Routledge, 1994), pp.56–68.
6. Todd Sandler and Walter Enders, 'Is Transnational Terrorism Becoming More Threatening?', *Journal of Conflict Resolution* 44:3, 2000, p.330.

POSTSCRIPT

1. Paul Virilio, *A Landscape of Events*, trans. Julie Rose (Cambridge, Mass.: MIT Press, 1996/2000), pp.18–19.
2. Paul Virilio, *The Information Bomb*, trans. Chris Turner (London: Verso, 1998/2000), pp.3 and 57. Apropos Virilio on science see also *The Open Sky* (London: Verso, 1997).
3. Paul Virilio, *Polar Inertia*, trans. Patrick Camiller (London: Sage, 1990/2000), p.3. For a description from Virilio about how cinema developed as a war instrument and became the arena of war see Paul Virilio, *War and Cinema*, trans. Patrick Camiller (London: Verso, 1984).
4. Paul Virilio, *The Vision Machine* (Bloomington and Indianapolis: Indiana University Press, 1994).
5. Raymond Aron, *Clausewitz: Philosopher of War*, trans. Christine Brooker and Norman Stone (London: Routledge & Kegan Paul, 1976), p.395.
6. Virilio, *The Information Bomb*, p.57.
7. Roland Barthes, *The Rustle of Language* (Oxford: Basil Blackwell, 1986).
8. Paul Virilio and Sylvère Lotringer, *Pure War*, trans. Mark Polizzotti (New York: Semiotext(e), 1983/1997), p.37.
9. Ibid., p.26.
10. Ibid., p.42.
11. Quoted from the *Guardian*, 4 December 2001, p.5.
12. Quoted from 'The Ashcroft Smear', *Washington Post*, 7 December 2001, p.A40.

13. James F. Hodge and Gideon Rose (eds), *How Did This Happen? Terrorism and the New War* (Oxford: Public Affairs Ltd, 2001) – especially the essays by Fouad Ajami, Karen Armstrong and Milton Bearden.

14. Fred Halliday, *Two Hours that Shook the World – September 11, 2001: Causes and Consequences* (London: Saqi, 2001).

15. These include *Sleepwalking Through History: The New World Order and Its Discontents* (London: Centre for the Study of Global Governance, LSE, 1993); *Islam and the Myth of Confrontation: Religion and Politics in the Middle East* (London: Tauris, 1996); *Revolution and World Politics: The Rise and Fall of the Sixth Great Power* (Durham, N.C.: Duke University Press, 1999); *The World at 2000* (New York: St. Martin's Press, 2000); and *Nation and Religion in the Middle East* (London: Saqi, 2000).

16. Halliday, *Two Hours*, p.49.

17. Ibid., pp.49–50.

18. Ibid., p.170.

19. Ibid., p.171.

Index